anatomy of
CYCLING

anatomy of
CYCLING

BLOOMSBURY

LONDON · NEW DELHI · NEW YORK · SYDNEY

Note

Whilst every effort has been made to ensure that the content of this book is as technically accurate and as sound as possible, neither the author nor the publishers can accept responsibility for any injury or loss sustained as a result of the use of this material.

Published by Bloomsbury Publishing Plc
50 Bedford Square
London WC1B 3DP
www.bloomsbury.com

First edition 2013

Copyright © 2013 Moseley Road Inc.

ISBN 978 1 4081 8769 2

A CIP catalogue record for this book is available from the British Library.

This book is produced using paper that is made from wood grown in managed, sustainable forests. It is natural, renewable and recyclable. The logging and manufacturing processes conform to the environmental regulations of the country of origin.

Printed and bound in China by Oceanic Graphic Printing (OGP)

10 9 8 7 6 5 4 3 2 1

CONTENTS

CONTENTS continued

INTRODUCTION:
FIT FOR CYCLING

As a cyclist, you already know how wonderful a bike ride can make your body feel. During a

good ride, your legs are pumping, your abdominal muscles are engaged, and a wide spectrum of

different muscles are working hard as you power forward.

But you can feel even better. When it comes to optimising performance, avoiding aches

and pains, and generally enhancing how you feel while cycling, there is always room for

improvement. This book will give you all the tools you need to condition your body for cycling.

Whether you are a beginner or a seasoned athlete, you can benefit from stretches,

strengthening moves that target your core and lower body, and exercises that improve your

posture and hone the sense of balance that is so vital to cycling effectively. The exercises in these

pages are designed to work a wide range of muscles that come into play when cycling. They

can be performed in your living room, so that in between forays into the streets or along the

mountain trails, you will be working your entire body to meet the unique demands of your sport.

FIT FOR CYCLING

Cycling is an incredibly rewarding activity. With its low impact on the joints and high rate of calorie burn, it is a great choice for anyone wanting to get (and stay) in shape. And it is accessible to enthusiasts of all fitness levels: no matter what your capability when beginning or returning to the sport, cycling allows for all forms of progression, from riding a flat mile in the local park loop to completing a first hilly 100-mile ride.

Cycling carries fantastic health benefits. It has been known to boost mental health, decrease the risk of coronary heart disease, and improve coordination skills. Studies have connected cycling to not only the physical effects of decreased waistlines and prolonged caloric burn, but also to heightened emotional health, mental capacity, and even earning potential and productivity at work.

If you're reading this book, you likely already have some level of interest in cycling. Perhaps you've seen the enviable chiselled quadriceps and calves of professional cyclists riding the Tour de France, or maybe you're looking for a low-impact transition from running.

You may simply love riding a bike and want to get better at it—or perhaps you want to try racing and are looking to increase speed and power output. Or maybe you're a triathlete and are seeking to help your current skills and capabilities transfer to the cycling portion of your racing.

Whatever the nature of your interest in cycling, this book will help you to get fit and stay fit for the physical demands of the sport. This is accomplished through targeting the muscles predominantly used to bring about forward motion of the bike, as well as through building the powerhouse muscles that will ultimately lead to a toned and balanced cycling body. After all, cycling is not all about the legs, but about core strength, balance, posture, and flexibility too.

Cyclists should be well-rounded athletes, recognising that strength on the bike draws from all the body's major and minor muscle groups. In the following pages, illustrations accompanying the step-by-step instructions will show you exactly which muscles you are working.

IMPROVING CYCLING PERFORMANCE

Starting out cycling or returning to the sport you loved as a child can be as simple as getting the bike in your garage tuned up and heading out for a spin. We all have different tolerances and capabilities when it comes to riding in vehicular traffic, and if you are not used to cycling, go first to a bike path or some other safe location before riding in the street. It is important to get comfortable with starting and stopping, scanning and signalling, and feeling the leaning and turning effects that come about when you cycle. Initially, if you stay at a reasonably low speed on flat terrain, you are unlikely to experience muscle fatigue; after all, the bike is an incredibly efficient machine.

It's more likely you'll experience some soreness in the back, knees, neck or even wrists and hands if the bike you're using was never properly fit to your body. The good news is that as long as your bike's frame is the right size (the bike shop can help you determine this), it is possible to adjust your body position so you do not feel aches and pains. Always give as much specific information as you can on what is hurting your body and where; front of the knee pain determines a different adjustment than back of the knee pain, for example.

Cycling fitness is determined largely by strength, cardiovascular endurance, muscle endurance, and power. Natural ability plays a role, but a well-trained, well-developed body can achieve even the most ambitious of goals. Whether you're a beginning cyclist or a Cat 1 racer, starting with a deep understanding of the body's interconnectedness is the first step in achieving goals. Simply riding more

FIT FOR CYCLING

miles, or faster miles, will not necessarily lead to a continuous improvement in fitness. It's more important to take a well-reasoned approach to your body's strengths and weaknesses, which in turn will allow you to craft a fitness plan that works for you.

Many areas of fitness can play a role in a cyclist's performance. Perhaps a beginner's goal is simply to complete a long ride, whatever that mileage may be. Perhaps a racer's goal is to have greater power output. Maybe a super-busy mother wants to pack as much intensity as possible into her short exercise sessions. With their targeted approach, the exercises in this book will prove effective for any cyclist wanting to develop endurance (whether cardiovascular or muscular), speed, and power.

It is a common misconception that cycling fitness is centred on the lower body: the quadriceps, hamstrings, and calves. Naturally a bike's forward motion is affected by the muscles in these groups, but development of the body as a whole will lead to balance, injury avoidance, and sustainability.

After all, few people enter the sport of cycling thinking it's for a short time. With proper muscle development and care, cycling is a sport that can and should be enjoyed well into your golden years. In fact, French cyclist Robert Marchand just set a record time for a 100-year-old when he rode 62 miles at a velodrome in Lyon.

A WELL-BALANCED APPROACH

Whether you're a beginner cyclist or have been riding for years, you already know that in order to ride a bike, you need to balance. Lean the bike too far one way or another and you'll likely find yourself falling. Failing to balance your body can lead to the same effect—an inability to keep cycling in the way you wish to cycle.

Be careful not to let your training become too one-sided. The repetitive position and mechanics of cycling can lead to imbalance in the body's development, and just like you will at some point consider upgrading your gear, it's important to consider upgrading your body's focus to include exercises that develop your body as a whole.

The proper development of musculature and balance will ensure that your new or longstanding interest doesn't give way to abandonment of the sport because you've developed chronic-use injuries or unmitigated aches and pains.

ADDUCTION VERSUS ABDUCTION

Have you ever sat hunched over your computer for an entire day? When you finally rise, the stretch that makes you feel better seeks to counteract the forward hunch. Maybe you lean, arms open, stretching back over your chair with your neck extended. Even if you are not feeling pronounced discomfort,

GETTING YOUR BIKE IN SHAPE

If you haven't ridden your bike in a year or more, before going out for that first ride, put your bike in the car and head first to your local bike shop and have a qualified mechanic give you a tune-up. Because the bike is a complex machine with many moving and integrated parts, there is an increased risk of injury when using a machine that is not in proper working order. Even if you're mechanically inclined, there are many subtle and not so subtle adjustments an experienced mechanic will make that will not only improve your overall

experience on the bike, but will increase your speed and efficiency. It's relatively easy to recognize a flat tyre, but far less easy to determine a loose and dangerous bottom bracket or head tube. And many components on new bikes have very specific tensions or torques where over-tightening could lead to dangerous failure or cause stress cracks and fractures.

Depending on the condition and age of your bike, expect to pay £30–£80 for a tune-up, which can include adjusting or replacing cables and housing,

overall cleaning of the entire frame and cassette, chain, cogs, lubricating the chain, overall inspection to adjust shifting and braking ability, replacement of brake pads, handlebar tape, or cracked and worn tyres.

A tune-up will typically take a few days, and should never be overlooked or substituted. Care will also be given to use proper lubricants specifically designed for bike parts; common household lubricant like WD-40 is neither intended for nor useful in cycling applications.

it often feels natural to counteract a prolonged body position by moving in the other direction. Too much of anything can lead to stress and strain.

Cycling is not unique in this respect. In other sports, where running, jumping, catching, or stretching are carried out over and over, different chronic-use injuries may come about. For instance, a tennis player may experience tendonitis in the elbow, while a basketball player may feel knee pain from running and jumping. In sports, the most common forms of injury involve the knees, neck, and back.

In cycling, discomfort can happen for many reasons. When you first start cycling, or begin again after a long break, some initial muscle soreness is normal, and often goes away. An improperly-fitting bike can also cause discomfort, as can

sitting in an uncomfortable position on the bike. But beyond these factors, repetitive motion is a major cause of imbalance and injury for cyclists.

This book specifically addresses how to counteract the effects of the repetitive motion associated with riding a bike. Exercises were specifically selected based on their characteristic of adduction verses abduction. Simply put, abduction is a motion that pulls a structure away from the

FIT FOR CYCLING

body, for example using the deltoid to raise the arms away from the side of the body. Adduction pulls a structure toward the body, as in squeezing the inner thighs together using the adductor longus muscles.

Utilising a careful balance of flexibility, abduction and adduction will lead to optimal cycling performance. Also, specifically choosing exercises such as Spinal Twist and Hamstring Stretch will target opposite motions as experienced on the bike.

"SPIN" VERSUS CYCLING

Spin, or spinning, is a form of indoor exercise offered in gyms, as a group class, held on exercise or stationary bikes. The kind of bikes can vary greatly, but usually are adjustable in many capacities and can include special pedals to accommodate "clip in"

cycling shoes. Spinning is experiencing a surge of popularity among cyclists and fitness enthusiasts due to its intense, sweat-producing workout and weather-benign indoor atmosphere. Many cyclists struggle to maintain their fitness through the winter when poor road conditions or lack of cold-weather gear keeps them off the bike for months at a time. Though cycling outdoors in winter can be enjoyable and safe, many people are not willing to manage the potentially (but not necessarily) substantial cost of special gear or the possibility of ice.

A typical spin class will include a pack of bikes facing one instructor's bike, often with loud or motivating music, and frequently occurs with the lights dimmed or at times turned off altogether. Since the bikes are not actually moving anywhere, the instructor will often use a microphone

to describe the "ride" participants may be on: imagery of flats, mountains, coasts, or especially beautiful scenery is invoked as bike tension is repeatedly self-altered to simulate hills, sprints, easy spinning, and recovery. Often the instructor, specifically trained in this kind of workout, will have participants sit and spin at a given pace (usually to the beat of the music), or will call for standing and pedalling or any given combination thereof.

When given an authentic effort, this workout can be intensely sweat-producing and exhausting, often a welcome effect in the cold of winter. The benefits naturally include development of cardiac capability and quadriceps strength. However, care should be taken to recognise that spin is not necessarily a good mimic of actual cycling. There is no balance employed, no true navigation of terrain, and at times the muscle-fatigue techniques of hovering over the bike seat by just a few inches is not comparable to the action that takes place on an actual bike. Additionally, the classes are often taught by trainers who are not cyclists, and while seeking to provide a good workout, they do not always provide a workout that benefits cycling goals. If you're considering taking a spin class, also consider wearing actual cycling gear; padded shorts can contribute a good deal towards comfort on the often-hard saddles.

For people who are interested in increasing their performance specifically in spin class, the exercises dedicated to strength and leg training will help develop optimal performance. Power Squat, Wall Sit, and Thigh Rock-Back are excellent choices for building strong legs. However, as with cycling outdoors, great care should be placed on developing balance in the body. Spin is a repetitive motion and it's possible to develop over-use injuries. Hamstring Stretch, Hand-to-Toe Lift, and Hip Flexor Stretch will be especially helpful in counteracting the motion of spin.

CYCLING AND NUTRITION

It's a common cycling adage to eat before you're hungry and drink before you're thirsty, and as a general rule this serves a good purpose. Because cycling is an endurance sport, it is critical to keep your body fuelleded. It is critically important to begin your workout hydrated and to stay that way throughout. Though experts disagree on the amount of fluids to be consumed during a work out, there is no disagreement that lack of proper hydration will lead to a dramatic decrease in ability and performance.

Nutrition is a science and a subject worthy of an entire book. People will choose foods for a variety of reasons while they cycle. Some choices are made based on sound scientific principles of

FIT FOR CYCLING

glycogen stores and uptake rates, while others will be made based on the body's tolerance for certain ingredients when under stress. There are supplements and easily convertible carbohydrate gels, or there are simple peanut butter sandwiches. The choice is personal and is best found through trial and error for your own goals.

A common misconception many beginners have concerns how much to eat during a ride. Generally, if you're going out for only an hour, don't stop for a calorie-rich peanut butter sandwich along the way. The body can store about 90 minutes worth of fuel to use. If your intention is less than that, it's not necessary to be overly concerned with consuming calories or using endurance drinks. However, it can be easily said that while riding, you should

be consuming carbohydrates. The body will extract glucose from carbohydrates much more easily than from protein or fat, so a high-fat choice of cream cheese on your bagel will only serve to make you feel sluggish. The body will be working hard to get the glucose out of the fat, while it works easily getting it from dried fruit or just a plain bagel. A good rule of thumb is to consume carbohydrates every 30 minutes while on a prolonged ride, even if you're not feeling hungry. If you choose to use a sports gel, remember to drink plenty of water when you consume it. Cheaper than sports gels is the simple jelly bean. It's easy to digest, high in carbohydrates, and simple to eat while riding.

Eating before you're hungry and drinking before you're thirsty are good rules to follow while riding, but what about after your ride? The first 30 minutes after your ride are absolutely critical to replenishing glycogen stores. Some experts recommend taking your weight and dividing that figure in half to determine the magic number of carbohydrate grams you should consume in this magic window after riding. The window for replenishing these stores is literally only 30–60 minutes, so make sure to have recovery foods readily available. An excellent and scientifically sound choice for after your ride is low fat chocolate milk. It's rich in carbohydrates and protein, needed to help refuel and repair muscles, but again should be consumed ideally within the first 30 minutes after finishing your workout.

You may find that it helps to designate an area of your home as a workout space. As much as possible, try to keep the space free of clutter and other distractions. It is all too easy to get caught up in thinking about phone calls you need to make, emails you need to return, and so on. But if you devote time to getting stronger and more flexible, you'll come to understand that the benefits merit the time spent away from your mobile phone. Exercising on a regular schedule helps to turn your home workout into a habit; even 15 minutes three times per week will go a long way toward improving your overall fitness—and, in turn, your experience and performance on the bike.

Medicine ball

YOUR HOME GYM

All of the exercises in this book were chosen not only to balance the body and optimise performance, but also to facilitate working out at home with minimal specialty equipment. Equipment used throughout the book consists of the following:

- a mat
- a chair
- a "Bosu ball"
- a small medicine ball
- a large Swiss ball
- a small roller
- a large roller

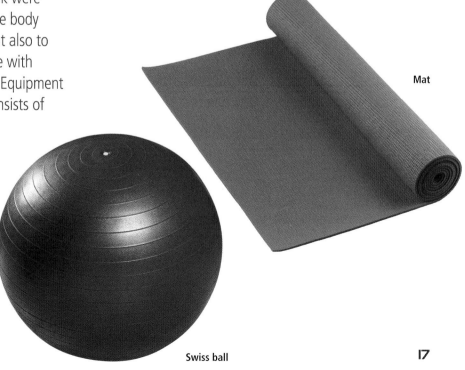

Mat

Swiss ball

FIT FOR CYCLING

BEYOND THE HOME GYM: CYCLING EQUIPMENT

There are as many different kinds of bikes as there are reasons for riding them. Bike types can be divided by function or sport. Though it's certainly possible to achieve health benefits from riding any kind of bike, some of the bikes used primarily for fitness are:

The differences between these kinds of bikes are primarily in the geometry of the frame design, materials used, and kinds of tyres that suit different terrains. A beginner cyclist may feel more stable to start out riding on a bike with a more upright geometry, or one that allows them

Mountain bike

Road bike

Cyclocross bike

Track bike

to put a foot flat on the ground without having to come off the saddle. As you increase the number of miles you're riding on the roads, you will notice the thicker, knobbier tyres of a mountain bike create a lot of rolling resistance. Road bikes, with their thin tyres, roll faster than the thicker mountain bike tyres, but are more delicate.

Deciding what kind of bike is best for you should be determined by asking a few basic questions:

• What kind of riding will you be doing? Will you be riding in lots of different terrains, or sticking to pavement?

• What is your budget? Bicycle costs can vary greatly from entry-level of a few hundred pounds to over £10,000. Remember too that the bike is not your only expense; you'll also need a helmet, gloves, eye protection, and possibly more depending on the kind of riding you're planning.

• What is your body type? Body shape and size may be a factor in choosing a bike. Someone who has a significant amount of weight to lose needs to be careful in considering weight limitations of wheels that come stock on already-built bikes. All bike shops can direct you to a sturdier wheel that is appropriate for heavier riders.

HOW TO USE THIS BOOK

In the following pages, you will find a wide variety of exercises, all selected to benefit you as a cyclist. Flexibility is vital, and the first section describes how to stretch your neck, your feet, and pretty much everything in between. You'll then move on to exercises that strengthen your legs in preparation for the demands of cycling; many exercises in this section work other parts of the body as well.

Next, you'll find an array of exercises to strengthen your core, that powerhouse of muscles including the abdominals, hip adductors, spinal extensors, and more, from which all bodily movement originates. And finally, you'll find moves that hone your posture and your sense of balance.

Follow the step-by-step instructions to ensure correct form, and review the anatomical illustrations that accompany each exercise to get a sense of which muscles you are targeting. Tips on performing the exercises correctly and advice on what to avoid will help you get the most of your workout, and lists of benefits, target muscles, and conditions which preclude certain exercises will enable you to choose a set of exercises that works best for your own needs.

UPPER-BODY ANATOMY

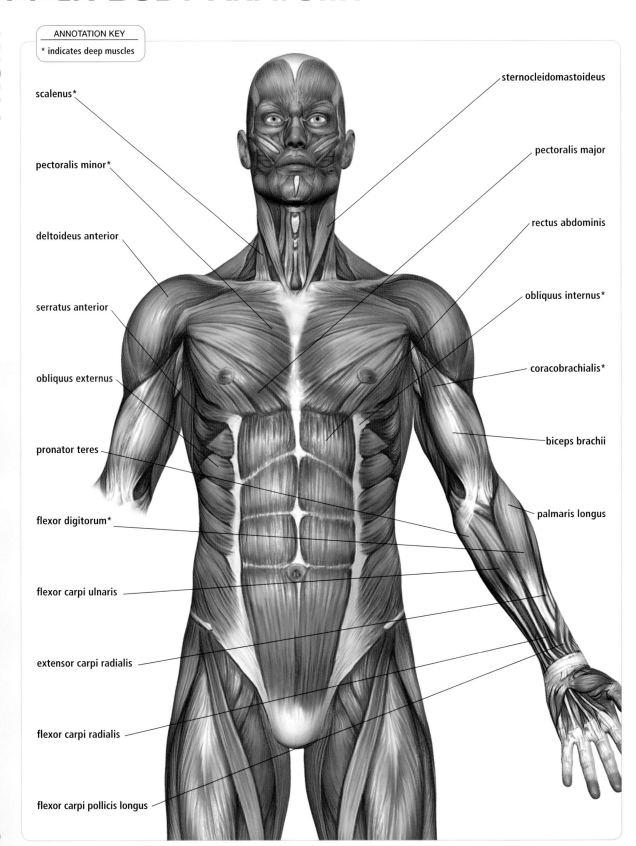

ANNOTATION KEY

* indicates deep muscles

scalenus*

pectoralis minor*

deltoideus anterior

serratus anterior

obliquus externus

pronator teres

flexor digitorum*

flexor carpi ulnaris

extensor carpi radialis

flexor carpi radialis

flexor carpi pollicis longus

sternocleidomastoideus

pectoralis major

rectus abdominis

obliquus internus*

coracobrachialis*

biceps brachii

palmaris longus

ANNOTATION KEY
* indicates deep muscles

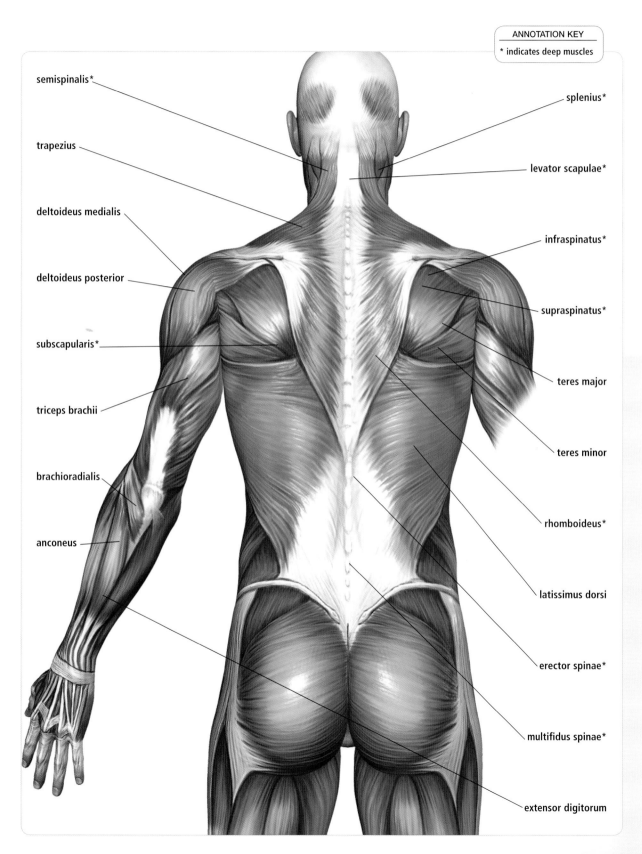

semispinalis*

trapezius

deltoideus medialis

deltoideus posterior

subscapularis*

triceps brachii

brachioradialis

anconeus

splenius*

levator scapulae*

infraspinatus*

supraspinatus*

teres major

teres minor

rhomboideus*

latissimus dorsi

erector spinae*

multifidus spinae*

extensor digitorum

LOWER-BODY ANATOMY

ANNOTATION KEY

* indicates deep muscles

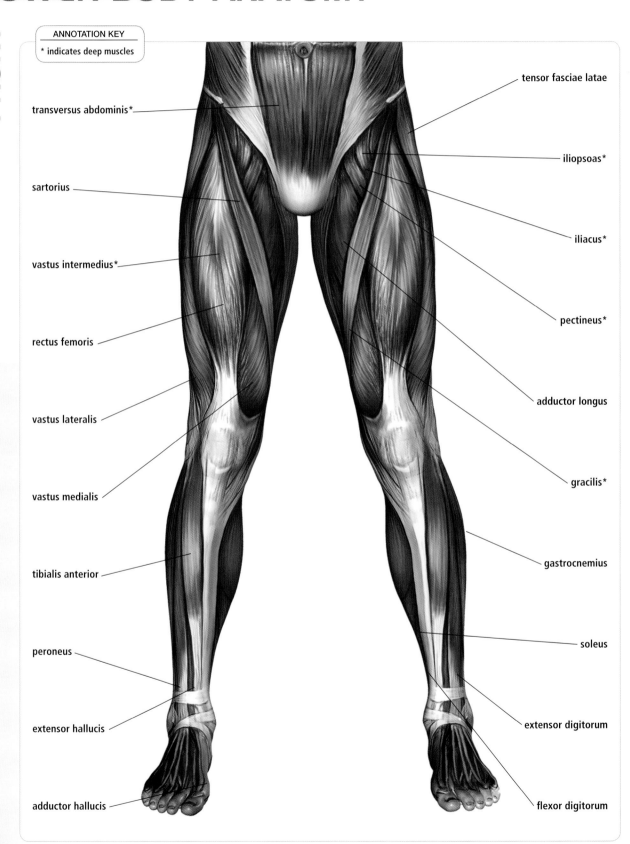

transversus abdominis*

sartorius

vastus intermedius*

rectus femoris

vastus lateralis

vastus medialis

tibialis anterior

peroneus

extensor hallucis

adductor hallucis

tensor fasciae latae

iliopsoas*

iliacus*

pectineus*

adductor longus

gracilis*

gastrocnemius

soleus

extensor digitorum

flexor digitorum

ANNOTATION KEY
* indicates deep muscles

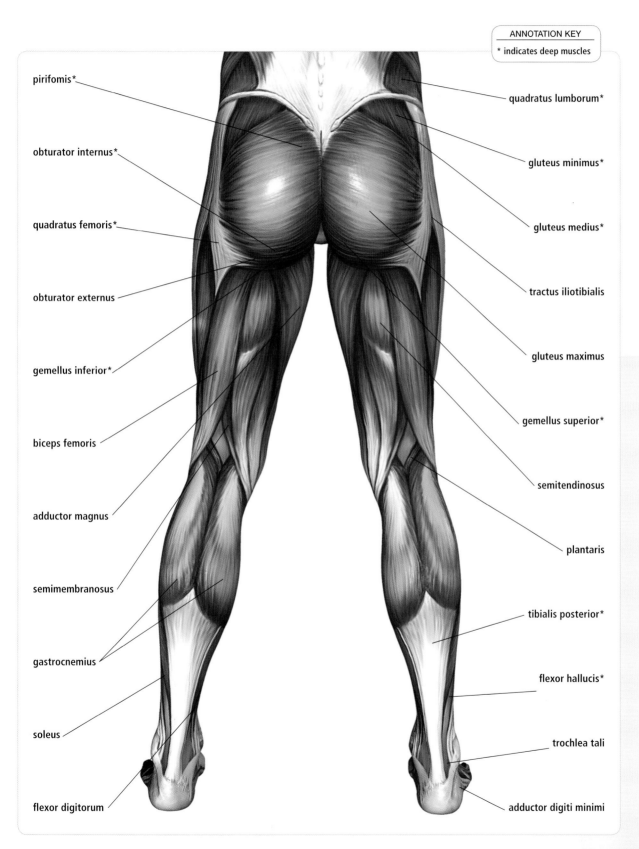

pirifomis*

obturator internus*

quadratus femoris*

obturator externus

gemellus inferior*

biceps femoris

adductor magnus

semimembranosus

gastrocnemius

soleus

flexor digitorum

quadratus lumborum*

gluteus minimus*

gluteus medius*

tractus iliotibialis

gluteus maximus

gemellus superior*

semitendinosus

plantaris

tibialis posterior*

flexor hallucis*

trochlea tali

adductor digiti minimi

FLEXIBILITY

Many aspiring and established athletes overlook the importance of flexibility; too often, getting the heart rate up through cardiovascular exercise or powering through a weight-lifting routine takes centre stage. But flexibility exercises carry immense benefits.

For cyclists, stretching plays an important role in counteracting stiffness. Performed consistently, holding a stretch for 15 seconds can dramatically increase range of motion, which in turn helps to decrease the risk of injury as muscles become more elastic. Stretching also increases blood flow so that more nourishment can reach muscles, and waste products that build up in working muscles, such as lactic acid, can be more effectively removed. The following exercises improve flexibility in your legs as well as your hips, abdominals, and gluteal muscles.

SPINAL TWIST

❶ Sit on the floor, with your back straight. Extend your legs in front of you, slightly more than hip-width apart.

❷ Lift yourself as tall as you can from the base of your spine. Ground your hips into the floor.

AVOID
• Allowing your hips to rise off the floor.

LOOK FOR
• Your torso to rotate along the central axis of your body.
• Your arms to remain parallel to the floor.

TARGETS
• Back flexibility

BENEFITS
• Strengthens and lengthens torso

NOT ADVISABLE IF YOU HAVE
• Back pain
• If your hamstrings are too tight to allow you to sit up straight, place a towel under your buttocks, and bend your knees slightly.

❸ Lift up and out of your hips as you pull in your lower abdominals. Twist from your waist to the left, keeping your hips squared and grounded.

❹ Slowly return to the centre.

❺ Lift up and out of your hips again, twisting in the other direction.

❻ Return to the centre. Repeat three times in each direction.

ANNOTATION KEY

Black text indicates target muscles

Gray text indicates other working muscles

* indicates deep muscles

BEST FOR

- transversus abdominis
- obliquus externus
- biceps femoris
- gluteus maximus
- tensor fasciae latae
- latissimus dorsi
- teres major
- quadratus lumborum
- deltoideus medialis
- rectus femoris

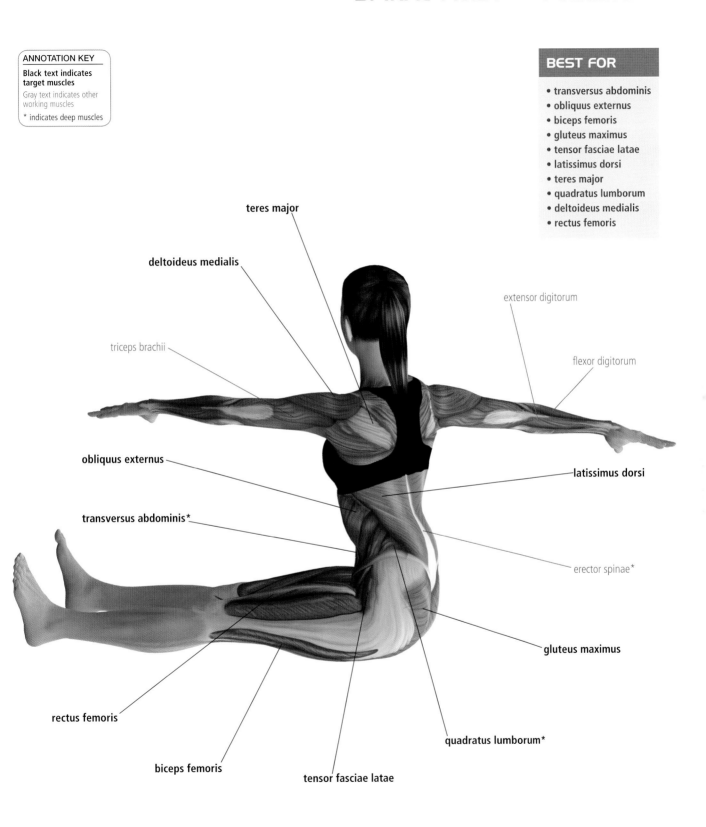

teres major

deltoideus medialis

triceps brachii

extensor digitorum

flexor digitorum

obliquus externus

transversus abdominis*

latissimus dorsi

erector spinae*

gluteus maximus

rectus femoris

biceps femoris

tensor fasciae latae

quadratus lumborum*

CHEST AND FRONT DELTOIDS STRETCH

BEST FOR

- pectoralis major
- pectoralis minor
- deltoideus anterior
- biceps brachii

① Stand straight with your arms behind your back and your hands clasped together.

② Pinch your shoulder blades together as you reach and lift your arms away from your body, making sure to keep your elbows straight.

③ Hold for 15 seconds before returning your arms to the starting position. Repeat.

LOOK FOR
- Your shoulders to remain pressed down, away from your ears.

TARGETS
- Chest
- Shoulders

AVOID
- Hunching your shoulders.
- Twisting your neck.

BENEFITS
- Stretches pectoral muscles and fronts of shoulders

ANNOTATION KEY
Black text indicates target muscles
Gray text indicates other working muscles
* indicates deep muscles

NOT ADVISABLE IF YOU HAVE
- Shoulder injury

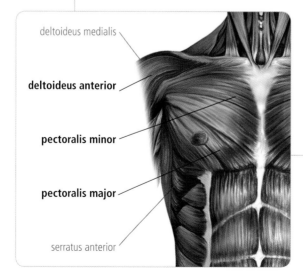

deltoideus medialis

deltoideus anterior

pectoralis minor

pectoralis major

serratus anterior

LATISSIMUS DORSI STRETCH

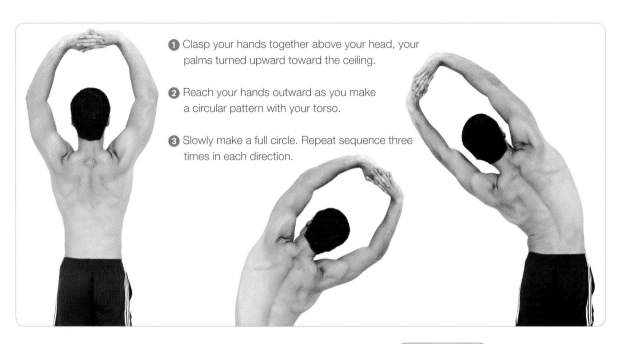

1. Clasp your hands together above your head, your palms turned upward toward the ceiling.

2. Reach your hands outward as you make a circular pattern with your torso.

3. Slowly make a full circle. Repeat sequence three times in each direction.

AVOID
- Leaning back as you come to the top of the circle.

LOOK FOR
- Your arms and shoulders to be elongated as much as possible.

ANNOTATION KEY
Black text indicates target muscles
Gray text indicates other working muscles
* indicates deep muscles

TARGETS
- upper back
- oblique muscles
- shoulders

BENEFITS
- Stretches back, obliques, and shoulders

NOT ADVISABLE IF YOU HAVE
- Shoulder injury

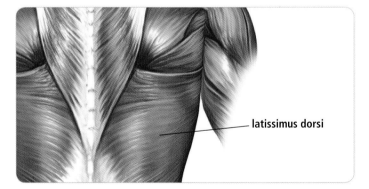

latissimus dorsi

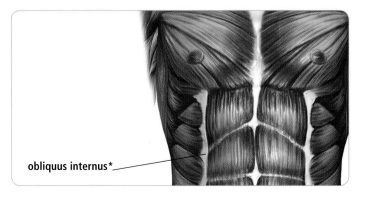

obliquus internus*

BEST FOR
- latissimus dorsi
- obliquus internus

SHOULDER STRETCH

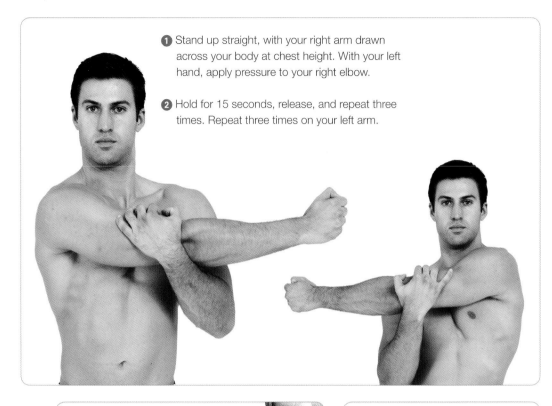

1 Stand up straight, with your right arm drawn across your body at chest height. With your left hand, apply pressure to your right elbow.

2 Hold for 15 seconds, release, and repeat three times. Repeat three times on your left arm.

TARGETS
• Shoulders

BENEFITS
• Stretches shoulders, preventing stiffness

NOT ADVISABLE IF YOU HAVE
• Shoulder injury

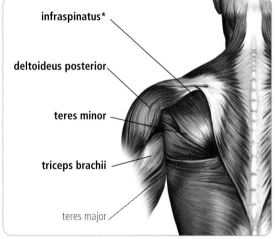

infraspinatus*

deltoideus posterior

teres minor

triceps brachii

teres major

obliquus externus

LOOK FOR
• Your elbow to remain straight while you apply pressure with your hand.

AVOID
• Allowing your shoulders to lift toward your ears.

ANNOTATION KEY
Black text indicates target muscles
Gray text indicates other working muscles
* indicates deep muscles

BEST FOR

• deltoideus posterior
• triceps brachii
• obliquus externus
• teres minor
• infraspinatus

TRAPEZIUS STRETCH

1 Standing with your feet parallel and shoulder-width apart, gently grasp the side of your head with your right hand.

2 Tilt your head toward your raised elbow until you feel the stretch in the side of your neck.

3 Turn your head toward your right shoulder, as you continue to feel the stretch.

4 Hold for 15 seconds, and repeat. Switch sides, and repeat the sequence on the left side.

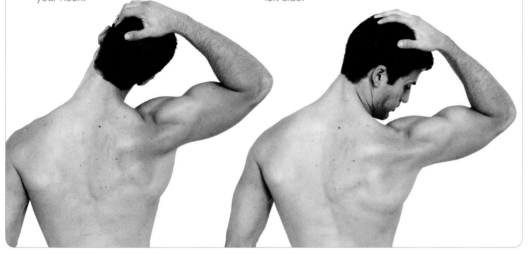

BEST FOR

- scalenus
- sternocleidomastoideus
- trapezius

ANNOTATION KEY

Black text indicates target muscles

Gray text indicates other working muscles

* indicates deep muscles

LOOK FOR
- The shoulder of your resting arm to remain pressed down, away from your ear.

AVOID
- Twisting your torso.

TARGETS
- Upper back

BENEFITS
- Stretches upper back and neck

NOT ADVISABLE IF YOU HAVE
- Shoulder injury

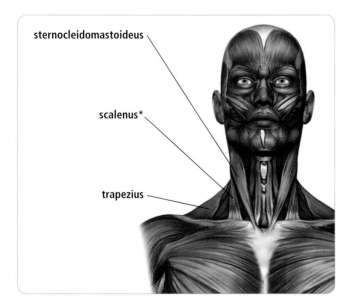

sternocleidomastoideus

scalenus*

trapezius

HIP FLEXOR STRETCH

1. Kneeling, bring one leg forward, with your foot in front of your knee.

2. Slowly lean forward and push your pelvis downward until you feel a stretch in the front of your hip. Hold for 15 seconds. Switch legs and repeat, completing the sequence three times on each leg.

BEST FOR
- rectus femoris
- vastus medialis
- biceps femoris
- tensor fasciae latae

TARGETS
- Hip flexors

BENEFITS
- Stretches hamstrings and hip flexors

NOT ADVISABLE IF YOU HAVE
- Hip injury
- Knee injury

AVOID
- Pushing your front knee past your ankle. The angle that your calf forms with the mat should not exceed 90 degrees.

LOOK FOR
- Your head to face forward and your back to remain straight.

ANNOTATION KEY

Black text indicates target muscles

Gray text indicates other working muscles

* indicates deep muscles

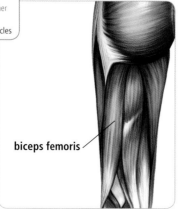

biceps femoris

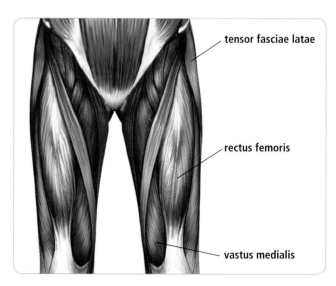

tensor fasciae latae

rectus femoris

vastus medialis

UPPER AND LOWER BACK STRETCH

LOOK FOR
- Your legs to remain in place, extended and on the floor.
- Your feet to maintain their 90-degree angle with your legs.
- Your forearms to rest slightly above your knees.

AVOID
- Leaning too far, too quickly; instead, stretch gradually.

1 Sit on the floor or on an exercise mat, with your legs extended in front of you, your ankles bent at a 90-degree angle so that your toes point toward the ceiling.

2 Loosely clasp your hands, and rest your forearms on your knees, bending your torso forward from your hips.

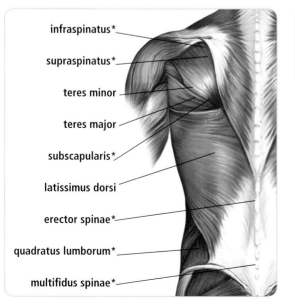

3 Without bouncing continue to lean forward, concentrating on stretching your entire spine.

4 Hold at your lowest point for about 15 seconds, and repeat.

TARGETS
- Back muscles
- Hamstrings

BENEFITS
- Stretches back and hamstrings

NOT ADVISABLE IF YOU HAVE
- Lower-back pain
- Neck injury

---

infraspinatus*

supraspinatus*

teres minor

teres major

subscapularis*

latissimus dorsi

erector spinae*

quadratus lumborum*

multifidus spinae*

ANNOTATION KEY
Black text indicates target muscles
Gray text indicates other working muscles
* indicates deep muscles

BEST FOR
- supraspinatus
- infraspinatus
- teres minor
- subscapularis
- teres major
- latissimus dorsi
- erector spinae
- quadratus lumborum
- multifidus spinae

SCOOP RHOMBOIDS

1. Sit on the floor and extend your legs in front of you in parallel position. Bend your knees slightly, keeping your heels on the floor.

2. Grasp beneath your hamstrings with your hands.

3. Keeping your chin down, round your upper back down as you lean back toward the floor. Hold for 10 to 15 seconds.

4. Slowly roll up to the starting position, and repeat if desired.

TARGETS
• Upper back

BENEFITS
• Stretches upper back
• Improves mobility in back muscles
• Reduces tension

NOT ADVISABLE IF YOU HAVE
• Lower-back pain

LOOK FOR
• Steady breathing. Focus on exhalation as you round your upper back and lean backward.

BEST FOR

• rhomboideus

ANNOTATION KEY

Black text indicates target muscles

Gray text indicates other working muscles

* indicates deep muscles

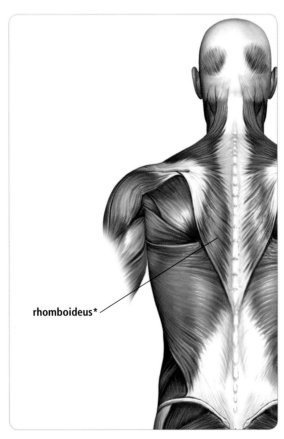

rhomboideus*

AVOID
• Holding your breath.

PIRIFORMIS STRETCH

1. Lie on your back with your knees bent.

2. Bring your left ankle over your right knee, resting it on your thigh. Place both hands around your right thigh.

3. Gently pull your right thigh toward your chest until you feel the stretch in your buttocks. Hold for 15 seconds and switch sides. Repeat sequence on your left leg.

TARGETS
• Gluteal muscles

BENEFITS
• Stretches hips and gluteal muscles, counteracting soreness

NOT ADVISABLE IF YOU HAVE
• Hip injury
• Knee injury

LOOK FOR
• Your hips to be relaxed so that you can go deeper into the stretch.
• The stretch to be performed slowly.

AVOID
• Rushing or forcing the stretch.

ANNOTATION KEY

Black text indicates target muscles

Gray text indicates other working muscles

* indicates deep muscles

BEST FOR

• piriformis
• gluteus maximus
• gluteus medius

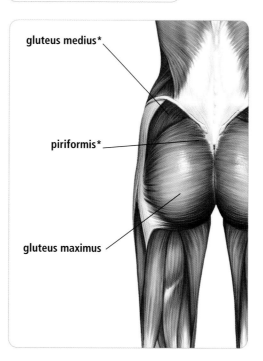

gluteus medius*

piriformis*

gluteus maximus

NECK STRETCHES

SIDE NECK TILT

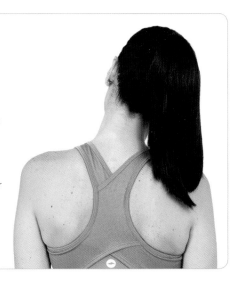

1. Stand with your legs and feet parallel and shoulder-width apart. Bend your knees very slightly.

2. Tuck your pelvis about ¼ inch forward and stand tall, with your chest slightly lifted and shoulders pressed lightly downward and back, away from your ears.

3. Slowly tilt your head to the right, feeling the weight of your head shifting in this direction as you hold for 5 seconds.

4. Slowly return your head to the centre, rest for 5 seconds, and repeat on the other side.

BEST FOR

• levator scapulae

TARGETS
• Neck

BENEFITS
• Stretches neck, counteracting stiffness

NOT ADVISABLE IF YOU HAVE
• Neck pain
• Severe neck stiffness

MODIFICATION
More difficult: Place the palm of one hand over your head with your fingertips touching your ear. Stretch your other arm downward, and extend your fingertips as if you were trying to grab something just out of reach.

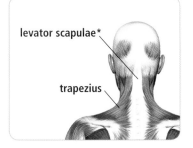

levator scapulae*

trapezius

BEST FOR

• trapezius

MODIFICATION
More difficult: To deepen this stretch, again place one hand on your head, and stretch your other arm downward.

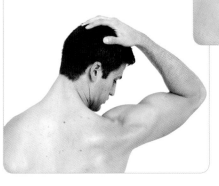

DOWNWARD NECK TILT

1. Still standing, look down, focusing your nose toward your armpit.

2. Hold for 5 seconds, return back to the neutral position, rest for 5 seconds, and repeat to the right for a second set.

AVOID
• Lifting or tensing your shoulders.

LOOK FOR
• Ease and normality of breathing as you stretch.

UPWARD NECK TILT

1. Still standing, slowly tilt your head so that your nose points toward the upper left. Focus your gaze upward.

2. Hold for 5 seconds.

3. Slowly return your head to the centre, rest for 5 seconds, and repeat on the other side.

BEST FOR

- sternocleidomastoideus
- splenius
- levator scapulae
- trapezius
- ligamentum interspinalis
- ligamentum capsular facet

UPWARD NECK TILT

1. Clasp your hands behind your head, interlacing your fingers. Gently tilt your head forward, and hold for 5 seconds.

2. Slowly bring your head back up, rest for 5 seconds, and repeat.

BEST FOR

- sternocleidomastoideus
- ligamentum nuchae
- ligamentum supraspinous
- trapezius

MODIFICATION

More difficult: Deepen the stretch by placing one hand on your head, and stretching the other arm downward.

BEST FOR

- sternocleidomastoideus

NECK AND HEAD TURN

1. Drop your hand and then lift your chin very slightly and focus straight ahead.

2. Turn your head to the right side, and hold for 5 seconds.

3. Slowly return your head to the centre, rest for 5 seconds, and repeat on the other side.

ANNOTATION KEY

Black text indicates target muscles

Gray text indicates other working muscles

Italic text indicates ligaments

* indicates deep muscles

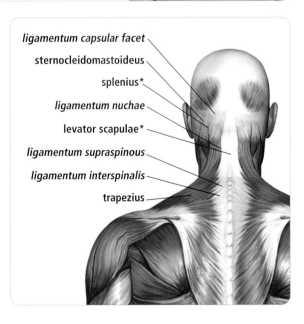

- *ligamentum capsular facet*
- sternocleidomastoideus
- splenius*
- *ligamentum nuchae*
- levator scapulae*
- *ligamentum supraspinous*
- *ligamentum interspinalis*
- trapezius

SPINE STRETCH

1 Lie on your back with your left leg straight and the right leg bent, placing your right foot on your left shin.

LOOK FOR
- Your lower back to remain relaxed.

2 Keeping both shoulders on the floor, slowly bring your right leg across your body until you feel the stretch in the area between your lower back and hips. Stretch only as far as your shoulders will allow without one of them rising from the floor.

3 Hold for 15 seconds, and repeat sequence three times on each side.

TARGETS
- Lower back
- Backs of thighs

BENEFITS
- Stretches lower back, hips, and thighs

NOT ADVISABLE IF YOU HAVE
- Hip injury
- Lower-back injury

BEST FOR
- quadratus lumborum
- erector spinae
- vastus lateralis
- tractus iliotibialis
- tensor fasciae latae

AVOID
- Allowing your shoulders to lift off the floor.

ANNOTATION KEY
Black text indicates target muscles
Gray text indicates other working muscles
* indicates deep muscles

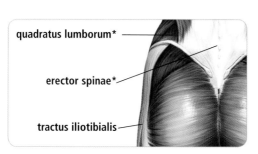

quadratus lumborum*

erector spinae*

tractus iliotibialis

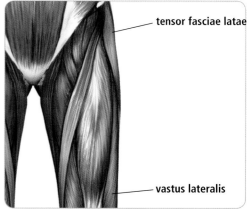

tensor fasciae latae

vastus lateralis

LUMBAR STRETCH

AVOID
- Allowing your shoulders to lift off the floor.

LOOK FOR
- Your lower back to remain relaxed.

BEST FOR
- quadratus lumborum
- erector spinae
- obliquus externus

1 Lie flat on the floor with both feet and knees together, your knees bent.

2 Slowly rock your knees from side to side until you feel a stretch along your lower back through the hips or until your knees reach the floor. Repeat ten times.

TARGETS
- Lower back

BENEFITS
- Stretches lower back, hips, thighs, and oblique muscles

NOT ADVISABLE IF YOU HAVE
- Hip injury
- Lower-back injury

ANNOTATION KEY

Black text indicates target muscles
Gray text indicates other working muscles
* indicates deep muscles

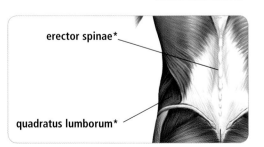

erector spinae*

quadratus lumborum*

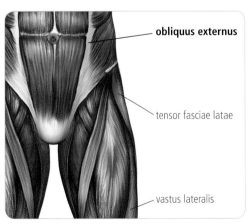

obliquus externus

tensor fasciae latae

vastus lateralis

HAMSTRINGS STRETCH

❶ Lie on your back with both knees bent and your feet flat on the floor.

❷ Grasp your left leg behind the knee, and draw your knee in toward your chest.

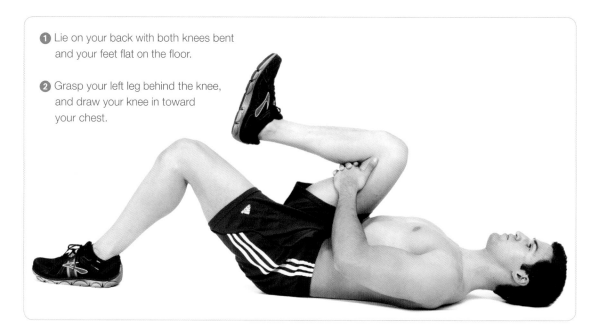

TARGETS
• Hamstrings
• Gluteal muscles

BENEFITS
• Stretches hamstrings and gluteal muscles

NOT ADVISABLE IF YOU HAVE
• Hip injury
• Knee injury

AVOID
• Rounding your shoulders and lifting your head.
• Rolling your stabilising leg out of neutral position.

LOOK FOR
• Your neck and shoulders to remain relaxed.
• Your knee to be pulled in toward the chest throughout the movement.
• Your toes to be flexed.

❸ Keeping your knee pulled into your chest, flex your toes and contract your quadriceps, so that you begin to straighten your leg.

❹ Release your leg into the stretch, and pull it closer toward your chest. Repeat ten times on each leg.

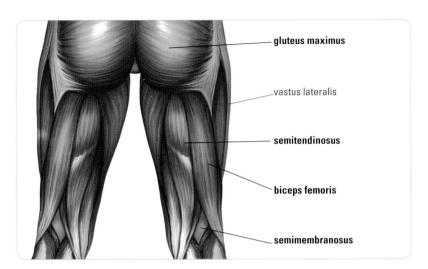

gluteus maximus

vastus lateralis

semitendinosus

biceps femoris

semimembranosus

ANNOTATION KEY

Black text indicates target muscles

Gray text indicates other working muscles

* indicates deep muscles

BEST FOR

- semitendinosus
- semimembranosus
- biceps femoris
- gluteus maximus

MODIFICATION

More difficult: Straighten your base leg so that it lies flat on the floor before drawing your other knee to your chest and then extending it.

1

2

CALF STRETCH

1 Stand with your feet parallel and close together, with your arms at your sides. Place a dumbbell on the floor in front of you.

2 Step forward to place the toes of your left foot on the dumbbell bar.

3 Lower your heel to the floor until you can feel a stretch.

4 Hold for 20 to 30 seconds, and repeat. Switch sides, and repeat on the right leg.

AVOID
• Twisting your hips.
• Arching your back or hunching forward.

LOOK FOR
• Your front foot to stay anchored on the dumbbell.
• Your hips to stay squared.

TARGETS
• Calf muscles

BENEFITS
• Stretches calf muscles

NOT ADVISABLE IF YOU HAVE
No restrictions

BEST FOR
• **gastrocnemius**
• **tibialis posterior**
• **soleus**
• **flexor digitorum**
• **flexor hallucis**

ANNOTATION KEY
Black text indicates target muscles
Gray text indicates other working muscles
* indicates deep muscles

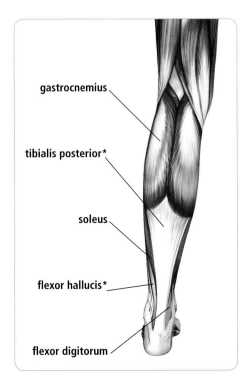

gastrocnemius

tibialis posterior*

soleus

flexor hallucis*

flexor digitorum

ILIOTIBIAL BAND STRETCH

① Standing, cross your left leg in front of your right.

AVOID
- Arching your back at any point.
- Forcing your hands to reach the floor.

LOOK FOR
- Your arms and legs to stay relatively straight.

② Bend at the waist while keeping both knees straight, and reach your hands toward the floor.

③ Hold for 15 seconds. Repeat sequence three times on each leg.

BEST FOR

- tractus iliotibialis
- biceps femoris
- gluteus maximus
- vastus lateralis

ANNOTATION KEY

Black text indicates target muscles

Gray text indicates other working muscles

* indicates deep muscles

TARGETS
- Iliotibial band

BENEFITS
- Stretches iliotibial band, calves, hamstrings, and glutes

NOT ADVISABLE IF YOU HAVE
- Back injury

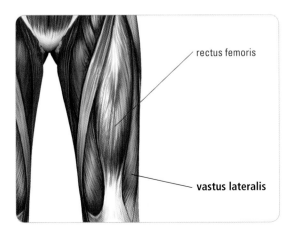

rectus femoris

vastus lateralis

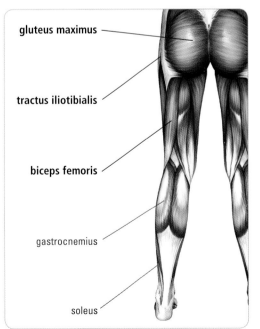

gluteus maximus

tractus iliotibialis

biceps femoris

gastrocnemius

soleus

HAND-TO-TOE LIFT

① Stand with both feet equally balanced on the floor, your shoulders relaxed but retracted back. Shift your weight onto your right foot.

② Raise your left leg toward your chest by bending your left knee. Grasp your toes with your left hand. Rest your right hand on your right hip.

BEST FOR

- rectus femoris
- vastus lateralis
- vastus medialis
- biceps femoris
- semitendinosus
- semimembranosus
- quadratus lumborum
- piriformis
- gemellus superior
- gemellus inferior
- tibialis anterior
- gracilis
- gluteus maximus

TARGETS
- Leg stability
- Abdominals

BENEFITS
- Strengthens legs and ankles
- Stretches backs of the legs
- Improves sense of balance

NOT ADVISABLE IF YOU HAVE
- Ankle injury
- Lower-back injury

LOOK FOR
- Your hips to be squared, facing forward—even when you raise your leg.
- Your torso to be lifted.

③ Extend your left leg, straightening it while pulling your foot inward as your extended leg moves to come in line with your torso.

④ Gaze at a single spot on the floor about a body's length in front of you. Flex your foot so that your toes curl back toward you. Hold for 5 seconds.

⑤ Lower your foot to the floor, and repeat five times on each side.

AVOID
- Moving your raised leg's hip up toward your lower ribs, so that your hips are no longer aligned.

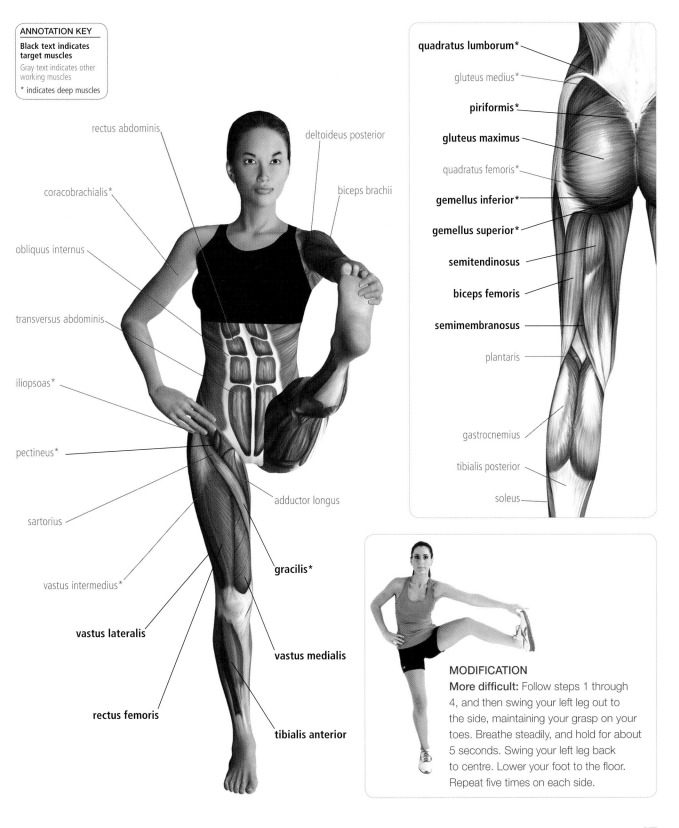

ANNOTATION KEY
Black text indicates target muscles
Gray text indicates other working muscles
* indicates deep muscles

rectus abdominis

coracobrachialis*

obliquus internus

transversus abdominis

iliopsoas*

pectineus*

sartorius

vastus intermedius*

vastus lateralis

rectus femoris

deltoideus posterior

biceps brachii

adductor longus

gracilis*

vastus medialis

tibialis anterior

quadratus lumborum*

gluteus medius*

piriformis*

gluteus maximus

quadratus femoris*

gemellus inferior*

gemellus superior*

semitendinosus

biceps femoris

semimembranosus

plantaris

gastrocnemius

tibialis posterior

soleus

MODIFICATION
More difficult: Follow steps 1 through 4, and then swing your left leg out to the side, maintaining your grasp on your toes. Breathe steadily, and hold for about 5 seconds. Swing your left leg back to centre. Lower your foot to the floor. Repeat five times on each side.

45

SHIN STRETCH

❶ Kneel with your buttocks resting lightly on your heels.

AVOID
• Arching your back.

TARGETS
• Shins
• Quadriceps

BENEFITS
• Stretches shins and quadriceps

NOT ADVISABLE IF YOU HAVE
• Lower-back pain

❷ Place your hands flat on the floor behind you, with your fingers pointing forward. Keep a slight bend in your elbows.

❸ Lean back slightly to increase the intensity of the stretch.

LOOK FOR
• Your gluteal muscles to be contracted and engaged to avoid a curve in your lumbar spine.
• A space to remain between the heels and the glutes.

BEST FOR

- gastrocnemius
- soleus
- rectus femoris
- vastus lateralis
- vastus intermedius
- vastus medialis
- tibialis anterior

ANNOTATION KEY

Black text indicates target muscles

Gray text indicates other working muscles

* indicates deep muscles

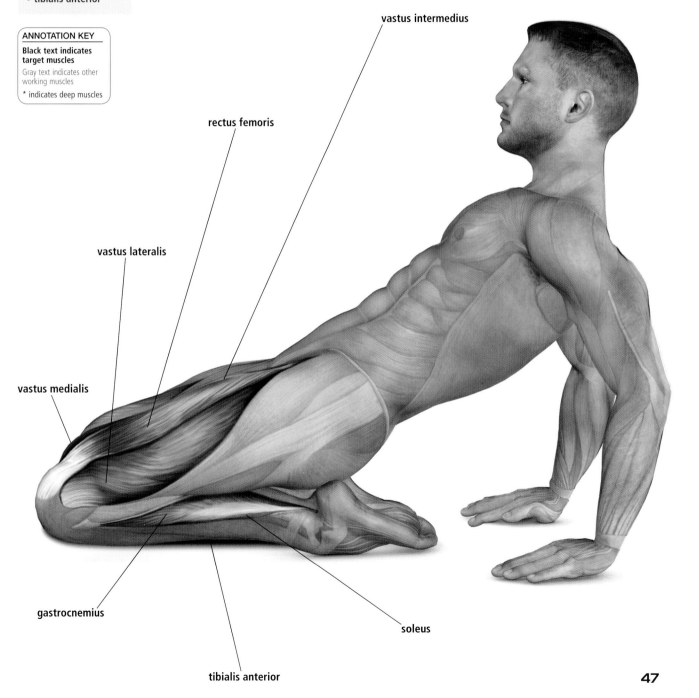

vastus intermedius

rectus femoris

vastus lateralis

vastus medialis

gastrocnemius

soleus

tibialis anterior

HAMSTRING-ADDUCTOR STRETCH

FLEXIBILITY

① Stand with your feet planted well beyond shoulder width apart, so that you are in a straddle position. Bend your knees.

② Place both hands on your left knee, keeping your spine in neutral position and your shoulders slightly forward.

③ Keeping your torso in the same position and your hips behind your heels, shift your weight to the left, bending your left knee while extending your right leg. Hold for 10 seconds and repeat on other side.

AVOID
• Arching your back, or hunching it forward.

BEST FOR

• adductor longus
• adductor magnus
• peroneus
• biceps femoris
• semitendinosus
• semimembranosus
• piriformis

TARGETS
• Hamstrings
• Inner thighs

BENEFITS
• Stretches hamstrings, gluteal muscles, and adductors

NOT ADVISABLE IF YOU HAVE
• Knee injury

ANNOTATION KEY
Black text indicates target muscles
Gray text indicates other working muscles
* indicates deep muscles

LOOK FOR
• Your hips to remain squared, facing forward.

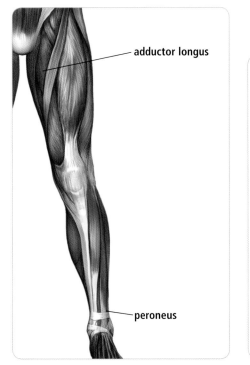

adductor longus

peroneus

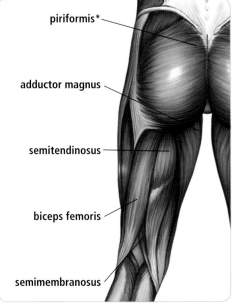

piriformis*

adductor magnus

semitendinosus

biceps femoris

semimembranosus

QUADRICEPS STRETCH

1. Stand with your feet parallel and close together, with your arms at your sides.

2. With your right hand, reach behind as you bend your right knee. Grasp your right foot and gently pull your heel toward your buttocks with your hand until you feel a stretch in the front of your thigh. Keep both knees together and aligned.

3. Hold for 15 seconds, and repeat. Switch sides, and repeat on the left leg.

BEST FOR

- rectus femoris
- vastus lateralis
- vastus medialis
- tensor fasciae latae

AVOID
- Twisting your torso or hips.
- Arching your back as you stretch.

LOOK FOR
- Your hips to remain squared.
- Your torso to stay upright.

TARGETS
- Quadriceps

BENEFITS
- Stretches fronts of thighs

NOT ADVISABLE IF YOU HAVE
- Knee injury

tensor fasciae latae

rectus femoris

vastus lateralis

vastus medialis

ANNOTATION KEY
Black text indicates target muscles
Gray text indicates other working muscles
* indicates deep muscles

ASSISTED FOOT STRETCHES

POINT

1 Sit on a chair or mat, and cross your right leg over the left so that your ankle rests on top of your left thigh.

2 Brace your right ankle with your right hand and grasp the front of your right foot with your left hand. Press down on the top of your foot, focusing the palm of your hand on the knuckles of your toes so that they point inward.

3 Switch legs, and repeat on the other side.

LOOK FOR
- Your palms to push forcefully during the slope-down phase—their downward force must be stronger than the upward force of your pulling fingers.
- Your fingers to push forcefully during the slope-up phase—their upward force must be stronger than the downward force of your pushing palms.

TARGETS
- Feet
- Calves
- Arch of the foot

BENEFITS
- Stretches feet, calves, and arches
- Strengthens ankles
- Improves range of motion in feet and calves
- Helps to prevent soreness, cramping, and other discomfort while pedalling

NOT ADVISABLE IF YOU HAVE
No restrictions

FLEXION

1 While still seated, again cross your right leg over the left so that your ankle rests on top of your thigh.

2 Brace your right heel with your right hand, and grasp the bottom of your toes and ball of the foot with your left hand.

3 Pull back on your toes until you feel a stretch in your arch.

4 Switch legs, and repeat on the other side.

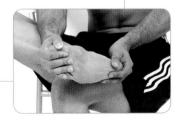

SLOPE-DOWN

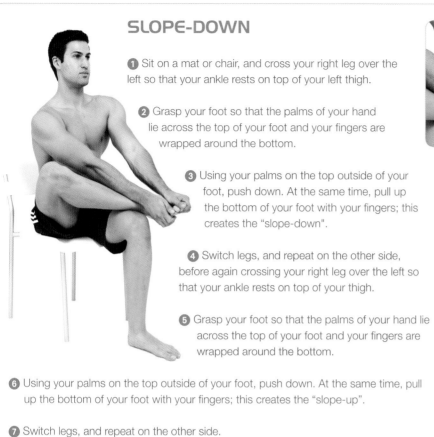

1. Sit on a mat or chair, and cross your right leg over the left so that your ankle rests on top of your left thigh.

2. Grasp your foot so that the palms of your hand lie across the top of your foot and your fingers are wrapped around the bottom.

3. Using your palms on the top outside of your foot, push down. At the same time, pull up the bottom of your foot with your fingers; this creates the "slope-down".

4. Switch legs, and repeat on the other side, before again crossing your right leg over the left so that your ankle rests on top of your thigh.

5. Grasp your foot so that the palms of your hand lie across the top of your foot and your fingers are wrapped around the bottom.

6. Using your palms on the top outside of your foot, push down. At the same time, pull up the bottom of your foot with your fingers; this creates the "slope-up".

7. Switch legs, and repeat on the other side.

SLOPE-UP

BEST FOR

- **extensor digitorum longus**
- **extensor digitorum brevis**
- **tibialis anterior**
- **extensor hallucis longus**
- **extensor hallucis brevis**
- **flexor digitorum brevis**
- **quadratus plantae**
- **flexor digiti minimi brevis**
- **flexor hallucis brevis**
- **lumbricales**
- **plantar interosseous**
- **abductor hallucis**
- **abductor digiti minimi**

AVOID
- Allowing your foot to shift—firmly stabilise your ankle and heel.

ANNOTATION KEY

Black text indicates target muscles

Gray text indicates other working muscles

* indicates deep muscles

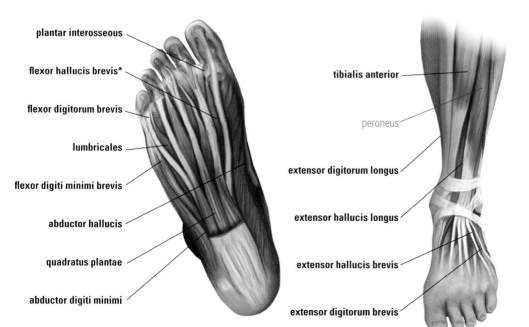

plantar interosseous

flexor hallucis brevis*

flexor digitorum brevis

lumbricales

flexor digiti minimi brevis

abductor hallucis

quadratus plantae

abductor digiti minimi

tibialis anterior

peroneus

extensor digitorum longus

extensor hallucis longus

extensor hallucis brevis

extensor digitorum brevis

BUTTERFLY STRETCHES

SEATED BUTTERFLY

1 Sit up tall on the floor or a mat, with the soles of your feet pressed together.

2 Place your forearms or elbows on your inner thighs, and grab your feet and toes with your hands.

3 Draw your heels in toward your core.

AVOID
• Slouching.
• Holding your breath.
• Rocking backward, off your hip bones; instead, feel them anchored on the floor.

TARGETS
• Adductors
• Lower back
• Trunk extensors

BENEFITS
• Stretches hips and lower back
• Prevents and counteracts soreness caused by long bike rides

NOT ADVISABLE IF YOU HAVE
• Hip issues
• Lower-back issues (Folded position)

FOLDED BUTTERFLY

1 From Seated Butterfly, place your forearms or elbows on your inner thighs, and grab your feet and toes with your hands. Keep your heels a comfortable distance from your core.

2 Fold your upper body forward until you feel a stretch in your groin and in your upper inner thighs.

3 Slowly roll up, and repeat if desired.

LOOK FOR
• Exhalation as you drop your chest toward the floor.

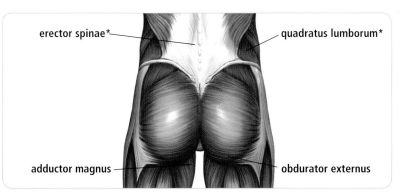

erector spinae*

quadratus lumborum*

adductor magnus

obdurator externus

ANNOTATION KEY

Black text indicates
target muscles

Gray text indicates other
working muscles

* indicates deep muscles

BEST FOR

- adductor longus
- adductor magnus
- adductor brevis
- gracilis
- pectineus
- obturator externus
- erector spinae
- quadratus lumborum

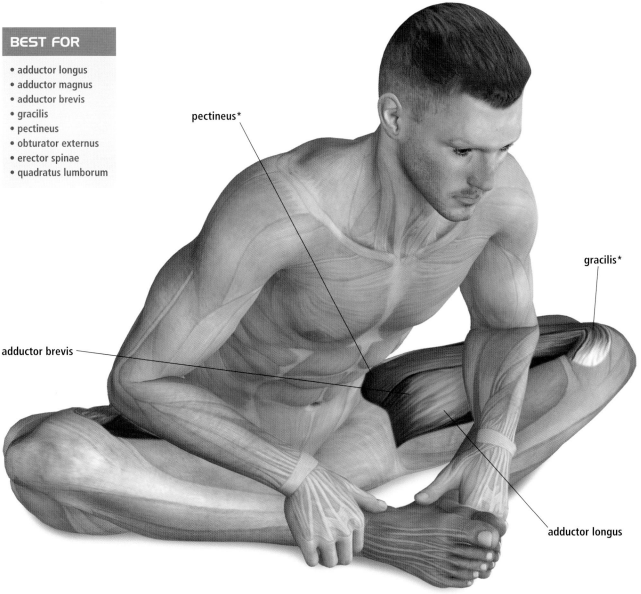

pectineus*

gracilis*

adductor brevis

adductor longus

LYING-DOWN FIGURE 4

① Lie on your back with your legs extended.

LOOK FOR
• Your head and shoulder blades to remain on the floor.

② Point both toes. Bend your right knee and turn the leg out so that your right ankle rests on your left thigh just above the knee, creating a figure 4.

TARGETS
• Gluteal muscles

BENEFITS
• Stretches muscles in gluteal region
• Prevents and counteracts soreness caused by long bike rides

NOT ADVISABLE IF YOU HAVE
• Hip issues

AVOID
• Twisting your lower body; instead, keep your hips square.

③ Bend your left leg, drawing both legs (still in the figure 4 position) in toward your chest as you grasp the back of your left thigh.

④ Push your right elbow against your right inner thigh, turning out the right leg slightly to increase the intensity of the stretch.

⑤ Return to the starting position, switch legs, and repeat.

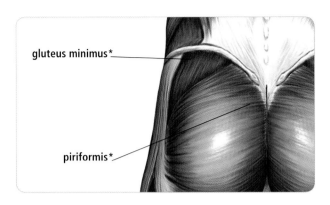

gluteus minimus*

piriformis*

BEST FOR

- gluteus maximus
- gluteus medius
- gluteus minimus
- piriformis

ANNOTATION KEY

Black text indicates target muscles

Gray text indicates other working muscles

* indicates deep muscles

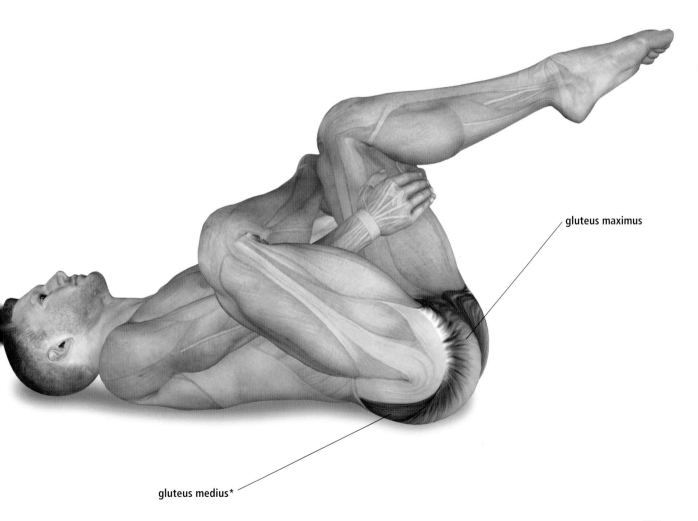

gluteus maximus

gluteus medius*

LEGS & ARMS

For cyclists, the benefits of building strong legs are evident. Strength translates naturally to power on the bike; speed is attained by pedalling faster—but without strength, important sprinting or hill-climbing skills will be lacking.

The following exercises will increase muscle strength, while also contributing to the development of bone strength that a cycling-only regimen lacks. What's more, supplementing your cycling with strengthening exercises like Thigh Rock-Back or the Clamshell Series, along with weight-bearing moves like Power Squat, counteracts the dreaded "plateau" effect that can occur when the same movement is carried out exclusively and repeatedly.

Quadriceps, gluteal muscles, hamstrings, and hip flexors are the primary muscles used in cycling, while strong arms also play a role. The following exercises will help you to build the strength you need to cycle to the best of your ability.

LATERAL LOW LUNGE

LOOK FOR
- Your spine to remain neutral as you bend your hips.
- Your shoulders and neck to remain relaxed.
- Your knee to align with the toe of your bent leg.
- The gluteal muscles to be tight as you bend.

AVOID
- Craning your neck as you perform the movement.
- Lifting your feet off the floor.
- Arching or extending your back.

TARGETS
- Gluteal and thigh muscles

BENEFITS
- Strengthens the pelvic, trunk, and knee stabilisers

NOT ADVISABLE IF YOU HAVE
- Sharp knee pain
- Back pain
- Trouble bearing weight on one leg

1 Stand upright with your hips and arms outstretched in front of you, parallel to the floor.

2 Step out to the left. Squat down on your right leg, bending at your hips, while maintaining a neutral spine. Begin to extend your left leg, keeping both feet flat on the floor.

3 Bend your right knee until your thigh is parallel to the floor, and your left leg is fully extended.

4 Keeping your arms parallel to the ground, squeeze your buttocks and press off your right leg to return to the starting position, and repeat. Repeat the sequence ten times on each side.

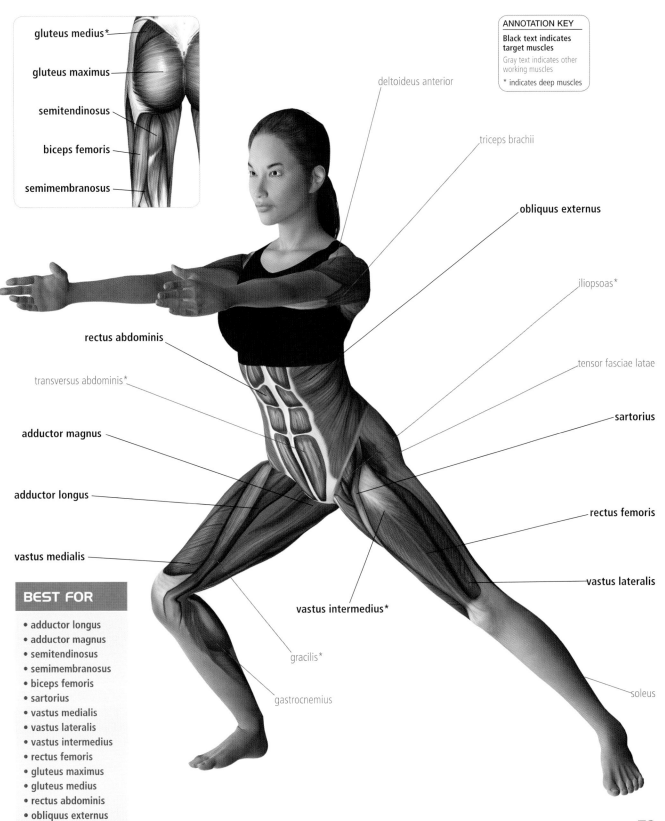

gluteus medius*

gluteus maximus

semitendinosus

biceps femoris

semimembranosus

ANNOTATION KEY
Black text indicates
target muscles
Gray text indicates other
working muscles
* indicates deep muscles

deltoideus anterior

triceps brachii

obliquus externus

iliopsoas*

rectus abdominis

transversus abdominis*

tensor fasciae latae

sartorius

adductor magnus

adductor longus

rectus femoris

vastus medialis

vastus lateralis

vastus intermedius*

gracilis*

gastrocnemius

soleus

BEST FOR

- adductor longus
- adductor magnus
- semitendinosus
- semimembranosus
- biceps femoris
- sartorius
- vastus medialis
- vastus lateralis
- vastus intermedius
- rectus femoris
- gluteus maximus
- gluteus medius
- rectus abdominis
- obliquus externus

FORWARD LUNGE

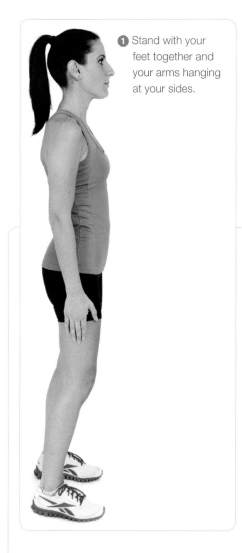

1 Stand with your feet together and your arms hanging at your sides.

LOOK FOR
• Proper position of your shoulders and your whole upper body, to help lengthen your spine.

AVOID
• Dropping your back-extended knee to the floor.

2 Exhale, and carefully step back with your right leg, keeping it in line with your hips as you step back. The ball of your left foot should be in contact with the floor as you do the motion.

3 Slowly slide your right foot farther back while bending your left knee, stacking it directly above your ankle.

4 Position your palms or fingers on the floor on either side of your left leg, and slowly press your palms or fingers against the floor to enhance the placement of your upper body and your head.

5 Lift your head and gaze straight forward while leaning your upper body forward and carefully rolling your shoulders down and backward.

6 Press the ball of your right foot gradually on the floor, contract your thigh muscles, and press up to maintain your left leg in a straight position.

7 Hold for 5 seconds. Slowly return to the starting position, and then repeat on the other side.

TARGETS
• Quadriceps
• Hamstrings
• Calf muscles

BENEFITS
• Strengthens legs and arms
• Stretches groins

NOT ADVISABLE IF YOU HAVE
• Arm injury
• Shoulder injury
• Hip injury
• High or low blood pressure

MODIFICATION

More difficult: Follow steps 1 through 3, using your right leg as the forward leg. Then position the palm of your left hand on the floor. Place your right hand behind your head, and slowly try to touch your elbow to the inside of your right ankle. Return to the starting position, and then repeat on the other side.

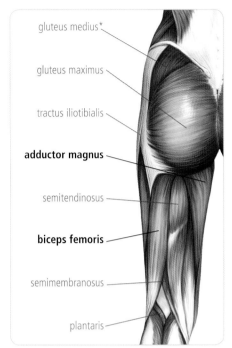

gluteus medius*

gluteus maximus

tractus iliotibialis

adductor magnus

semitendinosus

biceps femoris

semimembranosus

plantaris

BEST FOR

- **biceps femoris**
- **adductor longus**
- **adductor magnus**
- **gastrocnemius**
- **tibialis posterior**
- **iliopsoas**
- **rectus femoris**

ANNOTATION KEY

Black text indicates target muscles
Gray text indicates other working muscles
* indicates deep muscles

pectineus*

iliopsoas*

tensor fasciae latae

vastus lateralis

gastrocnemius

trapezius

soleus

adductor longus

vastus intermedius*

tibialis posterior*

rectus femoris

SIDE-LYING KNEE BEND

① Lie on your left side, with your legs extended together in line with your body. Extend your left arm, and rest your head on your upper arm.

② Bend your right knee and grasp the ankle with your right hand.

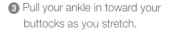

TARGETS
• Quadriceps

BENEFITS
• Stretches quadriceps

NOT ADVISABLE IF YOU HAVE
• Hip discomfort. If it feels uncomfortable to rest directly on the floor, place a towel under your bottom hip.

③ Pull your ankle in toward your buttocks as you stretch.

④ Return to the starting position, and repeat on the other side.

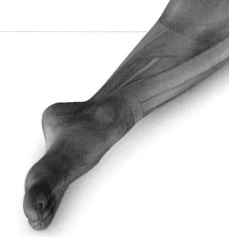

AVOID
• Leaning back onto your gluteal muscles.

LOOK FOR
• Your knees to stay together, one on top of the other.
• Your pelvis to be tucked slightly forward.
• Your chest to stay lifted, to engage and stretch your core.
• The foot of your bottom leg to stay pointed and parallel with your leg.

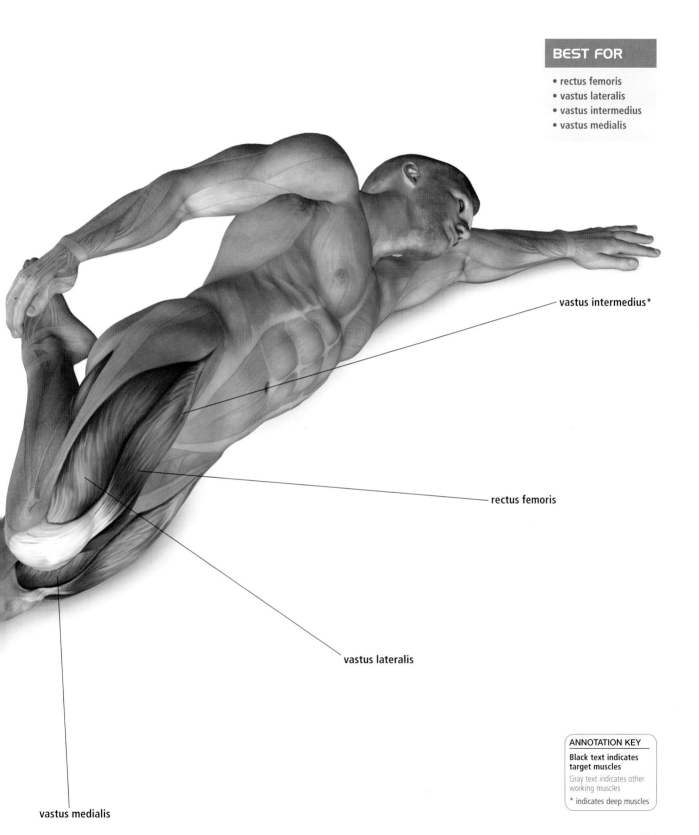

vastus intermedius*

rectus femoris

vastus lateralis

vastus medialis

BRIDGE WITH LEG LIFT

1 Lie in supine position on the floor, your arms by your sides and lengthened toward your feet. Your legs should be bent, with your feet flat on the floor.

2 Lift your hips and spine off the floor, creating one long line from your knees to your shoulders. Keep your weight shifted over your feet.

3 Keeping your legs bent, bring your left knee toward your chest.

TARGETS
- Hip extensor muscles
- Abdominals

BENEFITS
- Improves pelvic and spinal stability
- Increases hip flexor endurance

NOT ADVISABLE IF YOU HAVE
- Neck issues
- Knee injury

LOOK FOR
- Your hips and torso to remain stable throughout the exercise. If necessary, prop yourself up with your hands beneath your hips once you are in the bridge position.
- Your buttocks to remain tightly squeezed as you scoop in your abdominals for stability.

AVOID
- Allowing your back to do the work by extending out of your hips.
- Lifting your hips so high that your weight shifts onto your neck.

3 Keeping your legs bent, bring your left knee toward your chest.

4 Lower your left leg until your toe touches the mat. Be sure to keep your pelvis level.

5 Bring your left knee toward your chest again. Repeat sequence four to five times.

6 Lower your left leg to the floor, switch legs, and repeat the exercise with your right leg. Repeat sequence four to five times.

BEST FOR

- gluteus medius
- gluteus maximus
- rectus abdominis
- transversus abdominis
- quadratus lumborum
- biceps femoris
- iliopsoas
- rectus femoris
- sartorius
- tensor fasciae latae
- pectineus
- adductor longus
- gracilis

ANNOTATION KEY

Black text indicates target muscles

Gray text indicates other working muscles

* indicates deep muscles

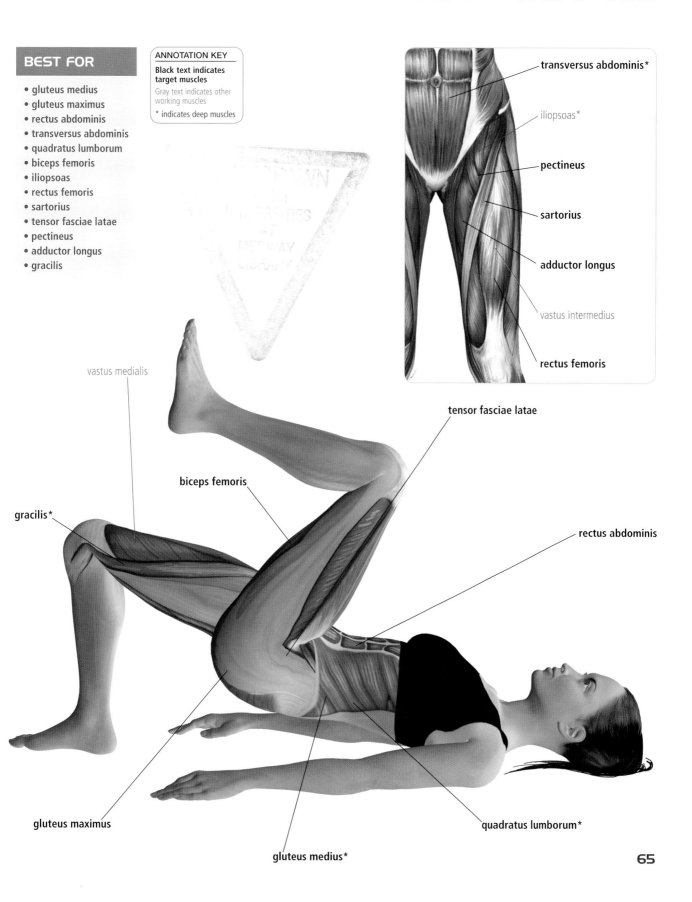

transversus abdominis*

iliopsoas*

pectineus

sartorius

adductor longus

vastus intermedius

rectus femoris

tensor fasciae latae

vastus medialis

biceps femoris

gracilis*

rectus abdominis

gluteus maximus

quadratus lumborum*

gluteus medius*

STEP DOWN

1 Standing up straight on a firm step or block, plant your left foot firmly close to the edge, and allow the right foot to hang off the side. Flex the toes of your right foot.

2 Lift your arms out in front of you for balance, keeping them parallel to the floor. Lower your torso as you bend at your hips and knees, dropping your right leg toward the floor.

AVOID
• Craning your neck.
• Placing weight on the foot being lowered to the floor—only allow a touch.

3 Without rotating your torso or knee, press upward through your left leg to return to the starting position. Repeat fifteen times for two sets on each leg.

TARGETS
• Quadriceps
• Gluteal muscles

BENEFITS
• Strengthens pelvic and knee stabilisers

NOT ADVISABLE IF YOU HAVE
• Ankle pain
• Sharp knee pain
• Sharp lower-back pain

LOOK FOR
• Your bent knee to align with your second toe—your knee should not rotate inward.
• Your knees and hips to move simultaneously as you bend.
• Your hips to remain behind your foot, leaning your torso forward as you lower into the bend.

66

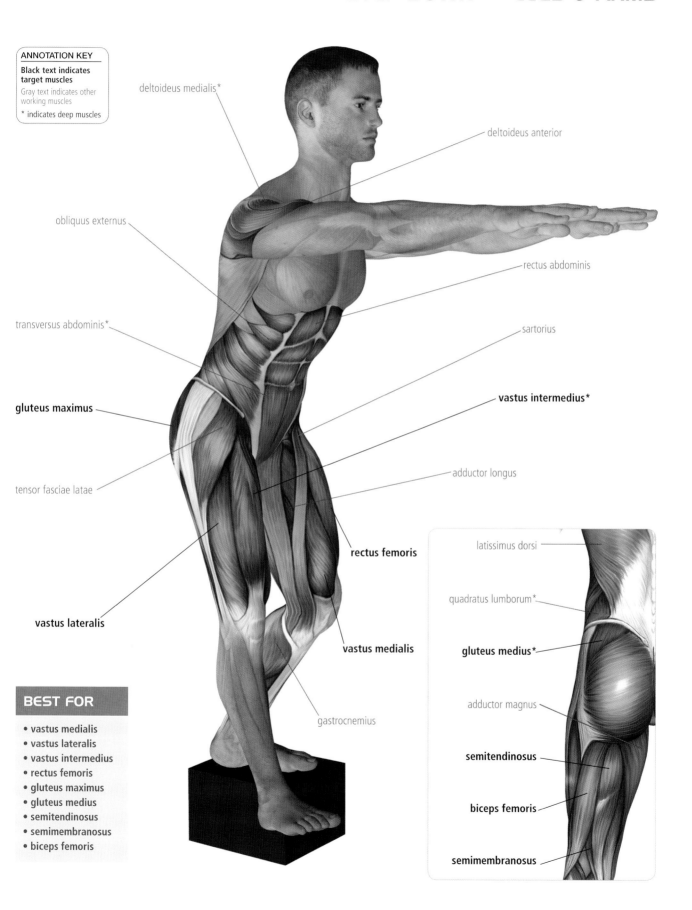

ANNOTATION KEY

Black text indicates target muscles

Gray text indicates other working muscles

* indicates deep muscles

deltoideus medialis*

deltoideus anterior

obliquus externus

rectus abdominis

transversus abdominis*

sartorius

gluteus maximus

vastus intermedius*

tensor fasciae latae

adductor longus

vastus lateralis

rectus femoris

vastus medialis

gastrocnemius

latissimus dorsi

quadratus lumborum*

gluteus medius*

adductor magnus

semitendinosus

biceps femoris

semimembranosus

BEST FOR

- vastus medialis
- vastus lateralis
- vastus intermedius
- rectus femoris
- gluteus maximus
- gluteus medius
- semitendinosus
- semimembranosus
- biceps femoris

WALL SIT

1. Stand with your back facing a wall. Lean against the wall, and walk your feet out from under your body until your lower back rests comfortably against it.

2. Slide your torso down the wall, until your hips and knees form 90-degree angles, your thighs parallel to the floor.

3. Raise your arms straight in front of you so that they are parallel to your thighs, and relax the upper torso. Hold for 1 minute, and repeat five times.

LOOK FOR
- Your body to remain firm throughout the exercise.
- Your shoulders and neck to remain relaxed.
- Your hips and knees to form 90-degree angles to receive maximum benefit from the exercise.

TARGETS
- Quadriceps
- Gluteal muscles

BENEFITS
- Strengthens quadriceps and gluteal muscles
- Trains the body to place weight evenly between legs

NOT ADVISABLE IF YOU HAVE
- Knee pain

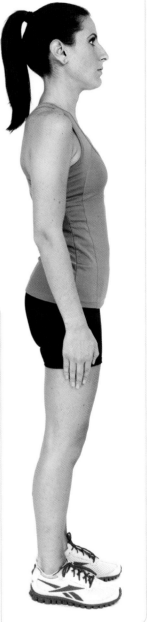

AVOID
- Sitting below 90 degrees.
- Pushing your back into the wall to hold yourself up.
- Shifting from side to side as you begin to fatigue.

BEST FOR

- vastus medialis
- vastus lateralis
- vastus intermedius
- rectus femoris
- semitendinosus
- semimembranosus
- biceps femoris
- gluteus maximus

obliquus externus

tensor fasciae latae

vastus intermedius*

vastus lateralis

tibialis anterior

tibialis posterior*

gastrocnemius

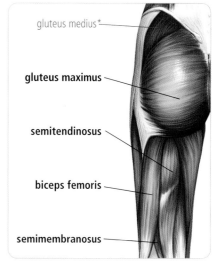

gluteus medius*

gluteus maximus

semitendinosus

biceps femoris

semimembranosus

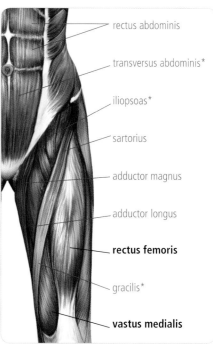

rectus abdominis

transversus abdominis*

iliopsoas*

sartorius

adductor magnus

adductor longus

rectus femoris

gracilis*

vastus medialis

CHAIR DIP

❶ Sit up tall near the front of a sturdy chair. Place your hands beside your hips, wrapping your fingers over the front edge of the chair.

❷ Extend your legs in front of you slightly, and place your feet flat on the floor.

❸ Scoot off the edge of the chair until your knees align directly above your feet and your torso will be able to clear the chair as you dip down.

❹ Bending your elbows directly behind you, without splaying them out to the sides, lower your torso until your elbows make a 90-degree angle.

❺ Press into the chair, raising your body back to the starting position. Repeat fifteen times for two sets.

TARGETS
• Triceps
• Shoulder and core stabilisers

BENEFITS
• Strengthens shoulder girdle
• Trains torso to remain stable while legs and arms are in motion

NOT ADVISABLE IF YOU HAVE
• Shoulder pain
• Wrist pain

MODIFICATION

More difficult: Keeping your knees squeezed together, perform the dips with one leg lifted straight out, parallel to the floor. Repeat fifteen times on each side.

LOOK FOR
- Your body to remain close to the chair.
- Your spine to remain neutral throughout the movement.

AVOID
- Allowing your shoulders to lift toward your ears.
- Moving your feet.
- Rounding your back at your hips.
- Pushing up solely with your feet, rather than using your arm strength.

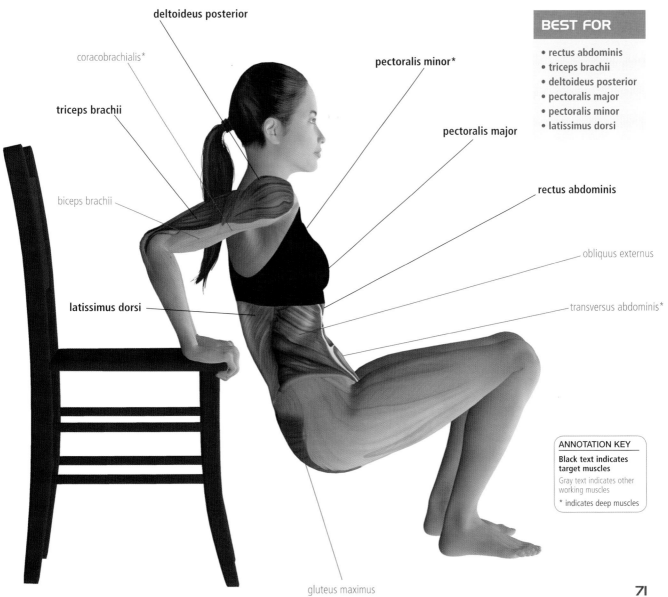

deltoideus posterior

coracobrachialis*

triceps brachii

biceps brachii

latissimus dorsi

pectoralis minor*

pectoralis major

rectus abdominis

obliquus externus

transversus abdominis*

gluteus maximus

BEST FOR

- rectus abdominis
- triceps brachii
- deltoideus posterior
- pectoralis major
- pectoralis minor
- latissimus dorsi

ANNOTATION KEY

Black text indicates target muscles

Gray text indicates other working muscles

* indicates deep muscles

PUSH-UP

① Stand straight, inhale, and pull your navel to your spine.

② Exhale as you roll down one vertebra at a time until your hands touch the floor in front of you.

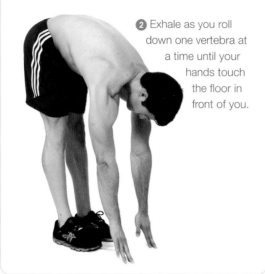

LOOK FOR
- Your neck to remain long and relaxed as you perform the push-up.
- Your buttocks to stay tightly squeezed as you scoop in your abdominals for stability.

③ Walk your hands out until they are directly beneath your shoulders in the plank position.

④ Inhale, and "set" your body by drawing your abdominals toward your spine. Squeeze your buttocks and legs together and stretch out of your heels, bringing your body into a straight line.

TARGETS
- Pectoral muscles
- Triceps

BENEFITS
- Strengthens core stabilisers, shoulders, back, buttocks, and pectoral muscles

NOT ADVISABLE IF YOU HAVE
- Shoulder issues
- Wrist pain
- Lower-back pain

⑤ Exhale and inhale as you bend your elbows and lower your body toward the floor. Then push upward to return to plank position. Keep your elbows close to your body. Repeat eight times.

⑥ Inhale as you lift your hips into the air, and walk your hands back toward your feet. Exhale slowly, rolling up one vertebra at a time into your starting position. Repeat the entire exercise three times.

MODIFICATIONS

Easier: Kneel with your hands on the floor in front of you, supporting your torso. Keeping your hips open, bend and straighten your elbows as if you were going to perform a push-up.

More difficult: Place your hands shoulder-width apart on an exercise ball. With the balls of your feet on the floor behind you, complete the push-up movement while maintaining stability on the ball.

More difficult: Place the balls of your feet on top of an exercise ball, while supporting your body with your hands on the floor in front of you. Use your abdominals to keep your body in a straight line and balance as you complete the push-up.

AVOID
• Allowing your shoulders to lift toward your ears.

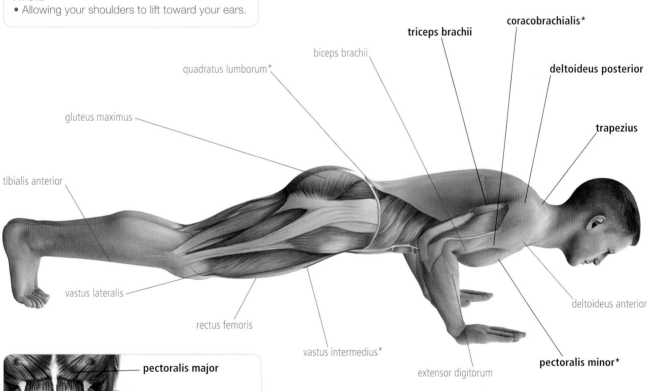

coracobrachialis*

triceps brachii

biceps brachii

deltoideus posterior

quadratus lumborum*

trapezius

gluteus maximus

tibialis anterior

deltoideus anterior

vastus lateralis

pectoralis minor*

rectus femoris

vastus intermedius*

extensor digitorum

pectoralis major

serratus anterior

rectus abdominis

obliquus internus*

obliquus externus

transversus abdominis*

iliopsoas*

BEST FOR

- triceps brachii
- pectoralis major
- pectoralis minor
- coracobrachialis
- deltoideus posterior
- rectus abdominis
- transversus abdominis
- obliquus externus
- obliquus internus
- trapezius

ANNOTATION KEY

Black text indicates target muscles

Gray text indicates other working muscles

* indicates deep muscles

ROLLER TRICEPS DIP

1. Sit on the floor with your legs outstretched, the foam roller behind you. Place both hands on the foam roller, with your fingers facing toward your buttocks, elbows bent.

2. Press through your legs and straighten your arms to lift your hips and shoulders.

LOOK FOR
- Your legs to remain firm with your knees straight.
- Your neck and shoulders to remain relaxed throughout the exercise.
- The roller to remain firmly pressed to the floor.

TARGETS
- Triceps
- Shoulder stabilisers
- Abdominals
- Hamstrings

AVOID
- Allowing your shoulders to lift toward your ears.
- Shifting the roller as you move up and down.

BENEFITS
- Improves core, pelvic, and shoulder stability

NOT ADVISABLE IF YOU HAVE
- Wrist pain
- Shoulder pain
- Discomfort in the back of the knee or knee swelling

3. Keeping your shoulders pressed down away from your ears, bend your elbows and dip your trunk up and down. The foam roller should not move. Repeat fifteen times for two sets.

deltoideus posterior

triceps brachii

serratus anterior

obliquus internus*

rectus abdominis

obliquus externus

transversus abdominis*

vastus lateralis

semimembranosus

biceps femoris

adductor magnus

quadratus lumborum*

gluteus medius*

gluteus maximus

semitendinosus

BEST FOR

- triceps brachii
- trapezius
- rhomboideus
- deltoideus posterior
- rectus abdominis
- transversus abdominis
- serratus anterior
- biceps femoris
- semitendinosus
- semimembranosus

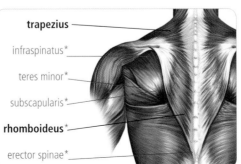

trapezius

infraspinatus*

teres minor*

subscapularis*

rhomboideus*

erector spinae*

ROLLER PUSH-UP

① Kneel on the floor with the roller placed crosswise in front of you. Place your hands on the roller with your fingers pointed away from you.

② Press into a plank position, lifting your knees and straightening your legs. Keep your hips level with your shoulders, and without allowing your shoulders to sink, bend your elbows and lower your chest to the roller. Avoid any roller movement throughout the motion.

③ Return to the starting position by pressing upward, straightening your elbows, and maintaining a straight spine. Repeat fifteen times for two sets.

TARGETS
- Triceps
- Shoulder stabilisers
- Abdominals

BENEFITS
- Improves core, pelvic, and shoulder stability

NOT ADVISABLE IF YOU HAVE
- Wrist pain
- Shoulder pain
- Lower-back pain

LOOK FOR
- A single plane of movement, with your body forming a straight line from shoulders to ankle.
- Your neck and shoulders to remain relaxed throughout the exercise.

AVOID
- Allowing your shoulders to lift toward your ears.
- Raising or lowering your body in segments.
- Bending your knees.

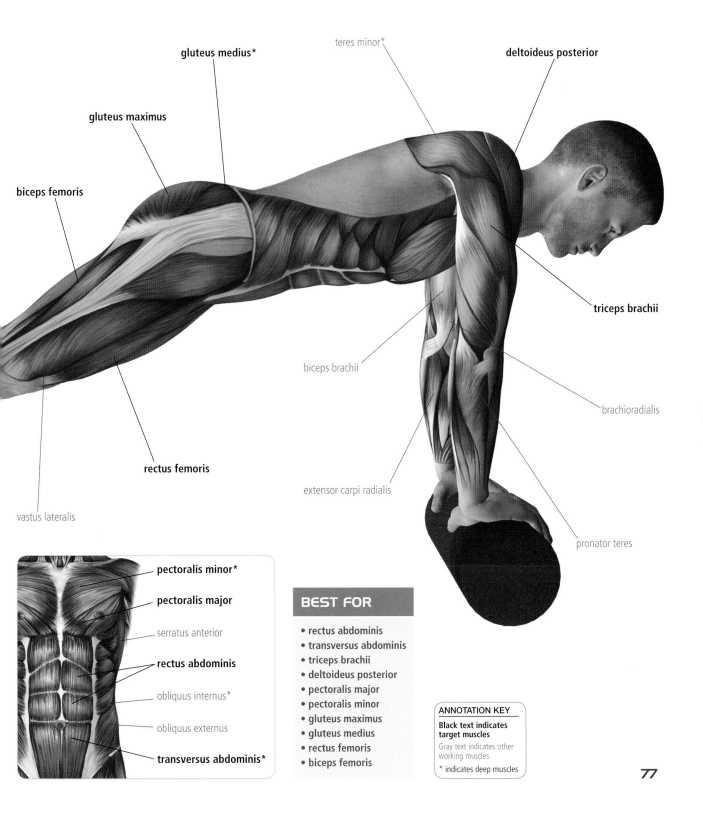

gluteus medius*

teres minor*

deltoideus posterior

gluteus maximus

biceps femoris

triceps brachii

biceps brachii

brachioradialis

rectus femoris

extensor carpi radialis

pronator teres

vastus lateralis

pectoralis minor*

pectoralis major

serratus anterior

rectus abdominis

obliquus internus*

obliquus externus

transversus abdominis*

BEST FOR

- rectus abdominis
- transversus abdominis
- triceps brachii
- deltoideus posterior
- pectoralis major
- pectoralis minor
- gluteus maximus
- gluteus medius
- rectus femoris
- biceps femoris

ANNOTATION KEY

Black text indicates target muscles

Gray text indicates other working muscles

* indicates deep muscles

POWER SQUAT

LOOK FOR
- The ball to create an arc in the air.
- Your hips and knees to be aligned throughout the movement.
- Your shoulders and neck to remain relaxed.

TARGETS
- Stabilisers of the body
- Gluteal and thigh strength

BENEFITS
- Improves balance
- Improves pelvic, trunk, and knee stabilisation
- Promotes stronger movement patterns

NOT ADVISABLE IF YOU HAVE
- Sharp knee pain
- Lower-back pain
- Shoulder pain

AVOID
- Allowing your knee to extend beyond your toes as you bend and rotate.
- Moving your foot from its starting position.
- Flexing your spine.

1. Stand upright, holding a weighted ball in front of your torso.

2. Shift your weight to your left foot, and bend your right knee, lifting your right foot toward your buttocks. Bend your elbows and draw the ball toward the outside of your right ear.

3. Maintaining a neutral spine, bend at your hips and knee. Lower your torso toward your left side, bringing the ball toward your right ankle.

4. Press into your left leg and straighten your knee and torso, returning to the starting position. Repeat fifteen times for two sets on each leg.

BEST FOR

- semitendinosus
- semimembranosus
- biceps femoris
- vastus medialis
- vastus lateralis
- rectus femoris
- gluteus maximus
- gluteus medius
- piriformis
- erector spinae
- tibialis anterior
- tibialis posterior
- soleus
- gastrocnemius
- infraspinatus
- supraspinatus

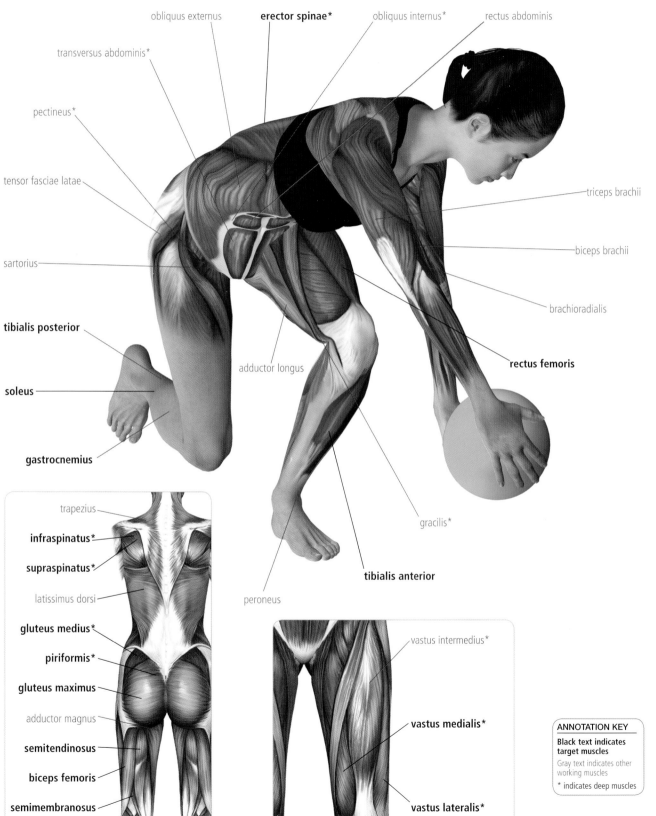

obliquus externus

erector spinae*

obliquus internus*

rectus abdominis

transversus abdominis*

pectineus*

tensor fasciae latae

triceps brachii

biceps brachii

sartorius

brachioradialis

tibialis posterior

rectus femoris

soleus

adductor longus

gastrocnemius

gracilis*

tibialis anterior

trapezius

peroneus

infraspinatus*

vastus intermedius*

supraspinatus*

latissimus dorsi

gluteus medius*

piriformis*

gluteus maximus

adductor magnus

vastus medialis*

semitendinosus

biceps femoris

semimembranosus

vastus lateralis*

ANNOTATION KEY

Black text indicates target muscles
Gray text indicates other working muscles
* indicates deep muscles

79

THIGH ROCK-BACK

① Kneel with your back straight and your knees hip-width apart on the floor, your arms by your sides. Pull in your abdominals, drawing your navel toward your spine.

AVOID
- Rocking so far back that you cannot return to the starting position.
- Bending in your hips.

② Lean back, keeping your hips open and aligned with your shoulders, stretching the front of your thighs.

③ Once you have leaned back as far as you can, squeeze your buttocks and slowly bring your body back to the upright position. Repeat four to five times.

TARGETS
- Quadriceps
- Abdominals

BENEFITS
- Stretches thighs
- Strengthens abdominals
- Increases range of motion of anterior ankle

NOT ADVISABLE IF YOU HAVE
- Quadriceps pain or injury

LOOK FOR
- A straight line to form between your torso and your knees.
- Your abdominals to work to control the movement.
- Your buttocks to be tight.

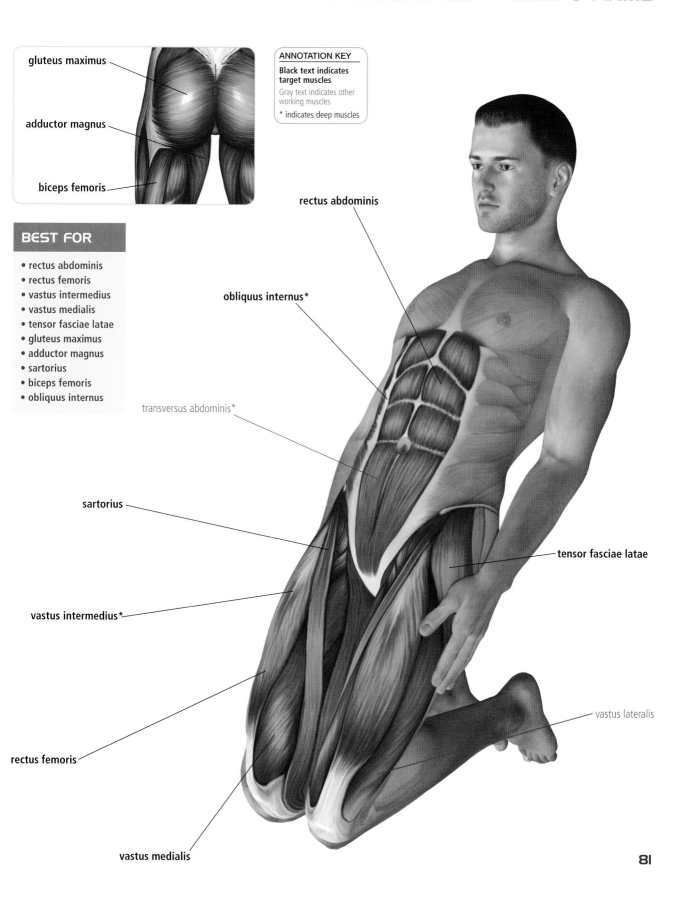

gluteus maximus

adductor magnus

biceps femoris

ANNOTATION KEY
Black text indicates target muscles
Gray text indicates other working muscles
* indicates deep muscles

BEST FOR

• rectus abdominis
• rectus femoris
• vastus intermedius
• vastus medialis
• tensor fasciae latae
• gluteus maximus
• adductor magnus
• sartorius
• biceps femoris
• obliquus internus

rectus abdominis

obliquus internus*

transversus abdominis*

sartorius

vastus intermedius*

rectus femoris

tensor fasciae latae

vastus lateralis

vastus medialis

SINGLE-LEG CIRCLE

1 Lie flat on the floor, with both legs and arms extended.

2 Bend your right knee toward your chest, and then straighten your leg up in the air. Anchor the rest of your body to the floor, straightening both knees and pressing your shoulders back and down.

AVOID
- Making your leg circles too big to maintain stability.

LOOK FOR
- Your hips and torso to remain stable while your legs are mobilised.
- Your raised leg to be elongated from your hip through your foot.

TARGETS
- Pelvic stability
- Abdominals

BENEFITS
- Lengthens leg muscles
- Strengthens deep abdominal muscles

NOT ADVISABLE IF YOU HAVE
- Snapping hip syndrome. If this is an issue, reduce the size of the circles.

3 Cross your raised leg up and over your body, aiming for your left shoulder. Continue making a circle with the raised leg, returning to the centre. Add emphasis to the motion by pausing at the top between repetitions.

4 Switch directions so that you aim your leg away from your body. Repeat with the other leg. Complete full movement five to eight times.

BEST FOR

- rectus abdominis
- obliquus externus
- rectus femoris
- biceps femoris
- triceps brachii
- gluteus maximus
- adductor magnus
- vastus lateralis
- vastus medialis
- tensor fasciae latae

ANNOTATION KEY

Black text indicates target muscles

Gray text indicates other working muscles

* indicates deep muscles

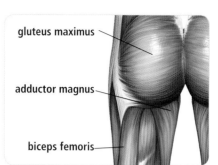

gluteus maximus

adductor magnus

biceps femoris

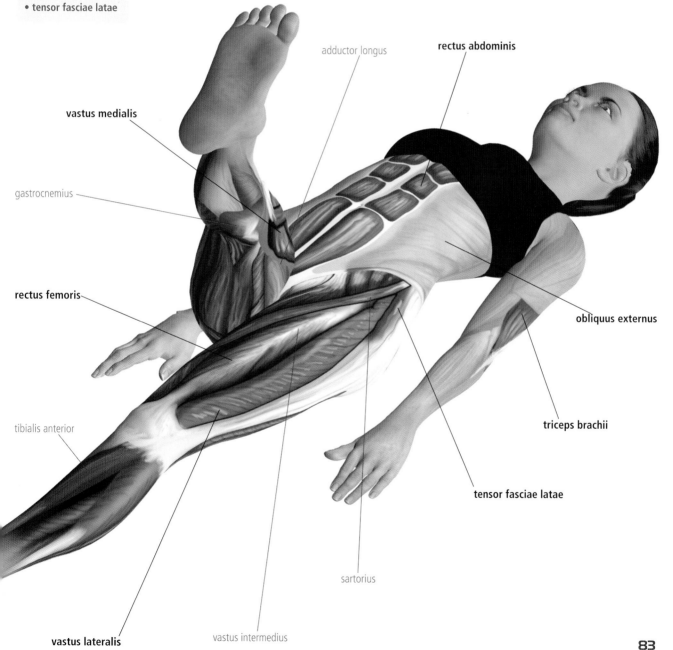

adductor longus

rectus abdominis

vastus medialis

gastrocnemius

rectus femoris

tibialis anterior

obliquus externus

triceps brachii

tensor fasciae latae

vastus lateralis

vastus intermedius

sartorius

CLAMSHELL SERIES

1 Lie on your right side with knees bent and stacked on top of each other. Bend your left elbow, placing it directly underneath your shoulder so that your forearm is supporting your upper body. Place your left hand on your hip.

AVOID
• Allowing your hips to move while lifting your knee.

LOOK FOR
• Your hips to be stacked and pulled forward slightly.
• Your shoulder and forearm to press into the floor throughout the exercise.
• Your neck and shoulders to be relaxed.

TARGETS
• Abdominals
• Abductor and adductor muscles
• Rotator cuff

BENEFITS
• Improves pelvic stability
• Strengthens abductor muscles
• Targets shoulder stabilisers for strengthening and endurance

NOT ADVISABLE IF YOU HAVE
• Shoulder injury
• Lower-back pain or injury

2 Without moving your hips, open your left knee upward, and then return to the starting position. Repeat ten times.

BEST FOR
• rectus abdominis
• obliquus internus
• obliquus externus
• tensor fasciae latae
• adductor magnus
• adductor longus
• iliopsoas
• gluteus medius
• quadratus lumborum

3 Lift both ankles off the floor, making sure to maintain a straight line with the torso.

4 While your ankles are still lifted, lift and lower your left knee to open and close your legs. Repeat ten times.

5 The final part of this series begins with both ankles elevated. Lift your left knee to separate your legs, and then straighten your left leg, being careful not to move the position of your thigh. Bend your knee and return to the starting position. Repeat ten times, switch sides, and start from the beginning.

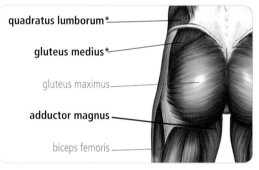

quadratus lumborum*

gluteus medius*

gluteus maximus

adductor magnus

biceps femoris

ANNOTATION KEY

Black text indicates target muscles

Gray text indicates other working muscles

* indicates deep muscles

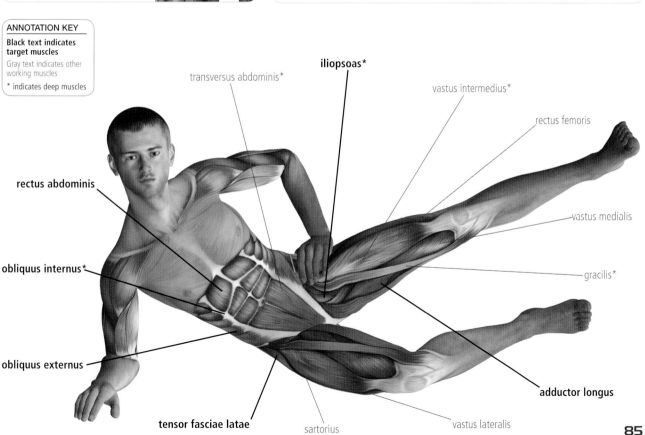

transversus abdominis*

iliopsoas*

vastus intermedius*

rectus femoris

rectus abdominis

vastus medialis

gracilis*

obliquus internus*

obliquus externus

adductor longus

tensor fasciae latae

sartorius

vastus lateralis

CORE STRENGTH & STABILITY

Although cycling may seem to be all about legs, having a strong and stable core is essential, too. When you cycle, the muscles around your pelvis, abdomen, hips, and lower back work together to contribute to a fluid pedal stroke. When these muscles are all balanced and working in concert, energy is isolated and focused through the body to the pedal, allowing you to ride with efficiency.

Your body is designed to stabilise before it engages in action, and these exercises will develop your body's ability to stabilise around your spine, which will ultimately bring about overall stability. When your core muscles are strong and engaged, your body naturally aligns to an effective and more-powerful pedalling action.

FRONT PLANK

① Sit with your legs parallel and stretched out in front of you. Place your hands behind you with your fingers pointed toward your hips.

LOOK FOR
- Your pelvis to remain elevated throughout the exercise.

TARGETS
- Hip extensor muscles
- Core stabilizers
- Arm muscles
- Leg muscles

BENEFITS
- Strengthens abdominals, arms, legs, and wrists
- Stabilises core
- Mobilises hips

NOT ADVISABLE IF YOU HAVE
- Wrist pain
- Knee pain
- Shoulder injury
- Shooting pains down leg

② Press up through your arms and lift your chest up, squeezing your buttocks and lifting your hips while pressing your heels into the floor. Continue lifting your pelvis until your body forms a long line from your shoulders to your feet.

AVOID
- Allowing your shoulders to sink into their sockets. If your legs do not feel strong enough to support your body, slightly bend your knees.

BEST FOR

- gluteus maximus
- biceps femoris
- deltoideus posterior
- rectus femoris
- adductor magnus
- tensor fasciae latae
- rectus abdominis
- transversus abdominis
- adductor longus
- obliquus externus
- latissimus dorsi
- triceps brachii

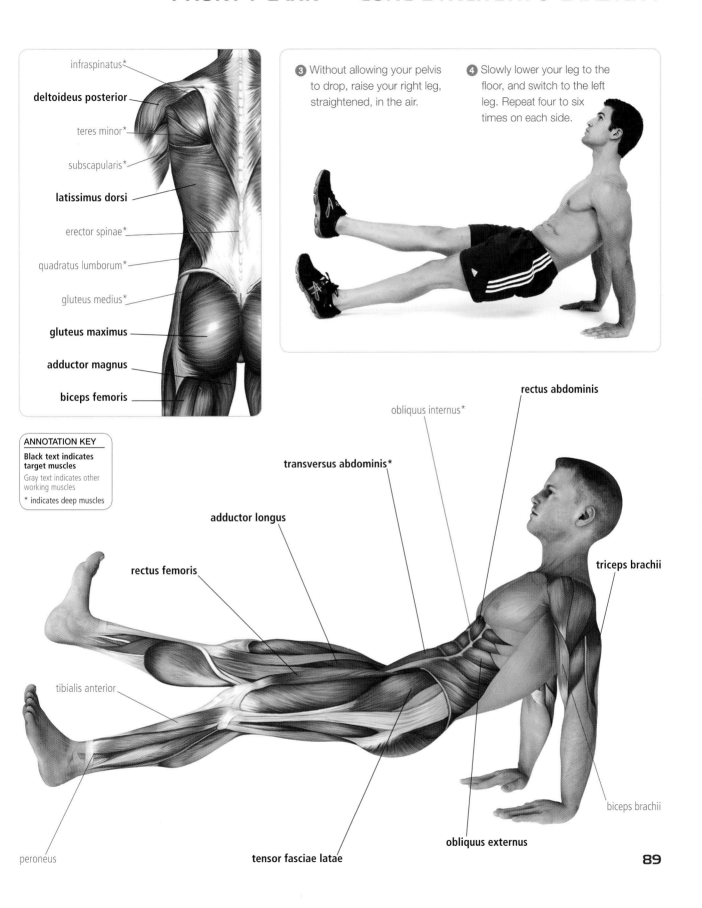

infraspinatus*

deltoideus posterior

teres minor*

subscapularis*

latissimus dorsi

erector spinae*

quadratus lumborum*

gluteus medius*

gluteus maximus

adductor magnus

biceps femoris

3 Without allowing your pelvis to drop, raise your right leg, straightened, in the air.

4 Slowly lower your leg to the floor, and switch to the left leg. Repeat four to six times on each side.

ANNOTATION KEY

Black text indicates target muscles

Gray text indicates other working muscles

* indicates deep muscles

rectus abdominis

obliquus internus*

transversus abdominis*

adductor longus

rectus femoris

triceps brachii

tibialis anterior

biceps brachii

peroneus

tensor fasciae latae

obliquus externus

SIDE PLANK BALANCE

❶ Begin in a plank position. Your arms should be straight with your wrists aligned under your shoulders.

AVOID
- Allowing your hips or shoulders to sway or sink.
- Lifting your hips too high.

TARGETS
- Chest muscles
- Core stability
- Abdominals, including obliques

BENEFITS
- Strengthens abdominals, arms, legs, and wrists
- Improves balance

NOT ADVISABLE IF YOU HAVE
- Shoulder issues
- Wrist injury
- Elbow injury

❷ Shift your weight onto the outside of your left foot and onto your left arm. Roll to the side, guiding with your hips and bringing your right shoulder back. Stack your right foot on top of the left, squeezing both legs together and straight.

LOOK FOR
- Your limbs to be as elongated as possible. While holding, stretch through your legs into the floor and reach your top arm to the ceiling.
- Your feet to be stacked and flexed, as if they were side by side in standing position.

3 Exhale, bring your right arm up to the ceiling, and elongate your body, making a straight line from your head to your heels. Gaze up at your fingertips as you continue to push through your shoulder into the floor, maintaining a strong balance.

4 Keep breathing as you hold the position for 15 to 30 seconds. Release, and then repeat on the other side.

BEST FOR

- rectus abdominis
- obliquus internus
- obliquus externus
- transversus abdominis
- pectoralis major
- pectoralis minor
- serratus anterior
- deltoideus anterior
- extensor digitorum

ANNOTATION KEY

Black text indicates target muscles

Gray text indicates other working muscles

* indicates deep muscles

pectoralis major

serratus anterior

deltoideus anterior

obliquus internus*

pectoralis minor*

transversus abdominis*

vastus intermedius*

rectus femoris

vastus lateralis

gastrocnemius

tibialis anterior

rectus abdominis

obliquus externus

iliopsoas*

palmaris longus

pectineus*

vastus medialis

adductor longus

extensor digitorum

SIDE-BEND PLANK

1. Lie on your right side with one arm supporting your torso, aligning the wrist under your shoulder. Place your left arm on top of your left leg. Your legs should be strongly squeezed together in adduction, with legs parallel and feet flexed. Draw your navel toward your spine.

TARGETS
- Triceps and pectoral muscles
- Abdominals, including obliques

BENEFITS
- Stabilises spine in neutral position with the support of shoulder girdle

NOT ADVISABLE IF YOU HAVE
- Rotator cuff injury
- Neck issues

LOOK FOR
- Your hips to be lifted high to take some weight off your upper body.
- Your limbs to be elongated as much as possible.

AVOID
- Allowing your shoulders to sink into their sockets or lift toward your ears.

2. Press into the palm of your right hand, and lift your hips off the floor, creating a straight line between your heels and head.

3. Slowly lower your hips, returning to the starting position. Repeat sequence five to six times, keeping your legs tight and buttocks squeezed. Repeat on other side.

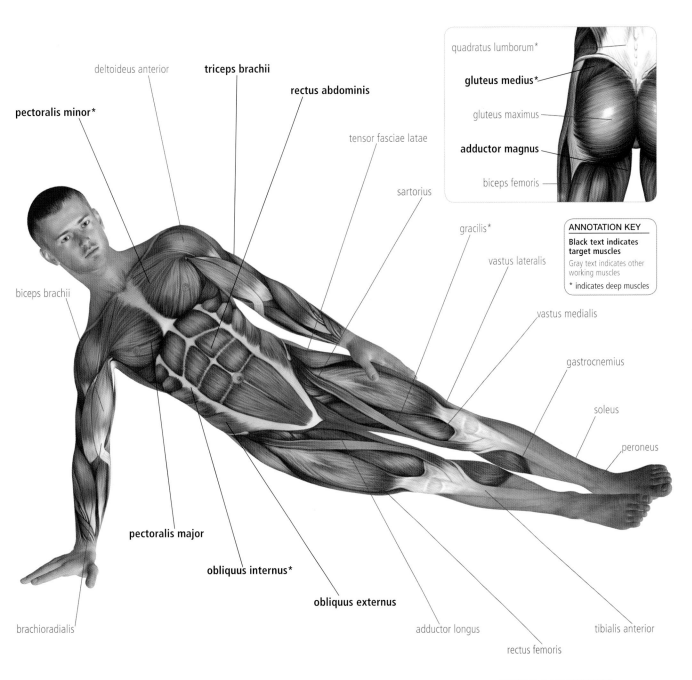

quadratus lumborum*

gluteus medius*

gluteus maximus

adductor magnus

biceps femoris

deltoideus anterior

triceps brachii

rectus abdominis

pectoralis minor*

tensor fasciae latae

sartorius

gracilis*

vastus lateralis

vastus medialis

gastrocnemius

soleus

peroneus

biceps brachii

ANNOTATION KEY

Black text indicates target muscles

Gray text indicates other working muscles

* indicates deep muscles

pectoralis major

obliquus internus*

obliquus externus

brachioradialis

adductor longus

rectus femoris

tibialis anterior

MODIFICATION

Easier: Rather than supporting your torso with your arm straight, bend your elbow so that it is aligned below your shoulder. Press into your forearm to lift your body into the side plank position.

BEST FOR

- rectus abdominis
- obliquus internus
- obliquus externus
- adductor magnus
- pectoralis major
- pectoralis minor
- triceps brachii
- gluteus medius

PLANK PRESS-UP

❶ Lying on the mat with your forearms underneath your chest, press your body up into a plank position, lengthening through your heels.

❷ Push through your forearms to bring your shoulders up toward the ceiling. With control, lower your shoulders until you feel them coming together in your back.

❸ Repeat five times.

TARGETS
• Scapular stabilisers
• Core stability

BENEFITS
• Strengthens core muscles
• Improves core stability
• Strengthens triceps
• Improves posture

NOT ADVISABLE IF YOU HAVE
• Shoulder injury
• Intense back pain

AVOID
• Allowing your back to sag.
• Allowing your shoulders to collapse into your shoulder joints.

LOOK FOR
• Lengthening through your neck.

BEST FOR
• deltoids
• rhomboideus
• rectus abdominis
• biceps brachii
• triceps brachii
• tensor fasciae latae
• rectus femoris
• transversus abdominis
• obliquus internus
• serratus anterior
• tibialis anterior

ANNOTATION KEY

**Black text indicates
target muscles**

Gray text indicates other
working muscles

* indicates deep muscles

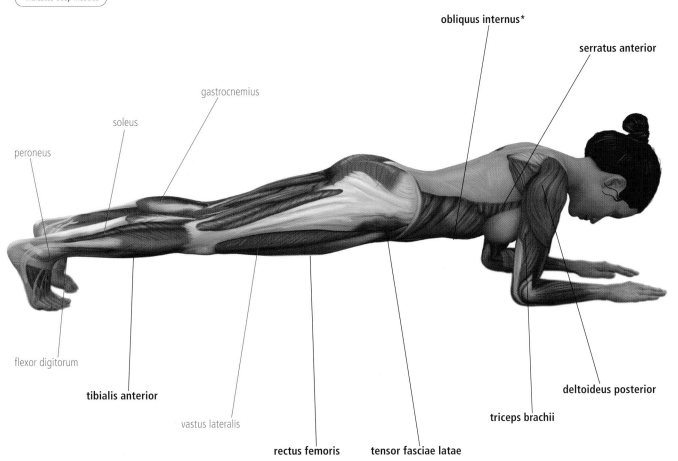

obliquus internus*

serratus anterior

gastrocnemius

soleus

peroneus

flexor digitorum

tibialis anterior

vastus lateralis

rectus femoris

tensor fasciae latae

triceps brachii

deltoideus posterior

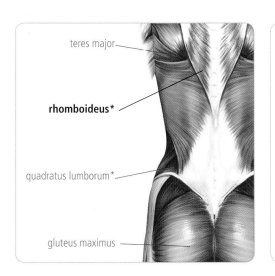

teres major

rhomboideus*

quadratus lumborum*

gluteus maximus

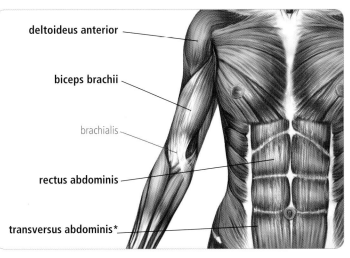

deltoideus anterior

biceps brachii

brachialis

rectus abdominis

transversus abdominis*

SINGLE-LEG KICK

① Lie prone on the mat with your arms flexed and elbows directly under your shoulders. Lengthen your legs and keep them adducted together.

TARGETS
• Hamstrings

BENEFITS
• Increases pelvic stability with hip extension

NOT ADVISABLE IF YOU HAVE
• Lower-back pain
• Problems with bending your knees

AVOID
• Allowing your lower back to sag.
• Kicking too hard.

LOOK FOR
• Drawing in your abdominals throughout the exercise.
• Sending the tailbone toward the floor.
• Keeping your shoulders and scapula down.
• Keeping the chest broad.

② Inhale, drawing your navel in toward your spine. Exhale, bending one knee. Point your foot and pulse your bent leg eight times.

③ Exhale, then flex your foot and pulse an additional eight times.

④ Inhale, straightening your bent leg on the mat next to the other leg. Exhale, bending your opposite leg, and repeat.

⑤ Repeat the entire sequence six to eight times.

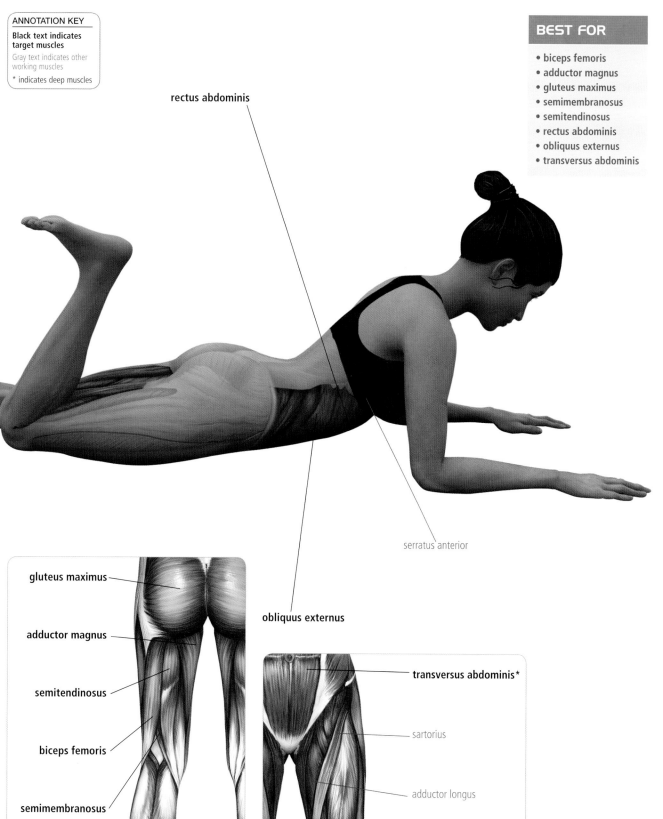

BEST FOR

- biceps femoris
- adductor magnus
- gluteus maximus
- semimembranosus
- semitendinosus
- rectus abdominis
- obliquus externus
- transversus abdominis

rectus abdominis

serratus anterior

gluteus maximus

adductor magnus

semitendinosus

biceps femoris

semimembranosus

obliquus externus

transversus abdominis*

sartorius

adductor longus

SCISSORS

1 Lie with your back on the floor, your arms by your sides and your legs raised in a tabletop position. Inhale, drawing in your abdominals.

BEST FOR

- biceps femoris
- rectus femoris
- tensor fasciae latae
- rectus abdominis
- obliquus externus

2 Reach your legs straight up, and lift your head and shoulders off the floor. Hold the position while lengthening your legs.

3 Extending your right leg away from your body, raise your left leg toward your trunk. Hold your left calf with your hands, pulsing twice while keeping your shoulders down.

TARGETS
- Abdominals

BENEFITS
- Increases stability with unilateral movement
- Increases abdominal strength and endurance

NOT ADVISABLE IF YOU HAVE
- Tight hamstrings. If this is an issue, you may bend the knee that is moving toward your chest.

4 Switch your legs in the air, reaching for your right leg. Stabilize your pelvis and spine. Repeat sequence six to eight times on each leg.

AVOID
- Bending your leg.

LOOK FOR
- Your legs to be as straight as possible.
- Your navel to be drawn into your spine.

ANNOTATION KEY

Black text indicates target muscles

Gray text indicates other working muscles

* indicates deep muscles

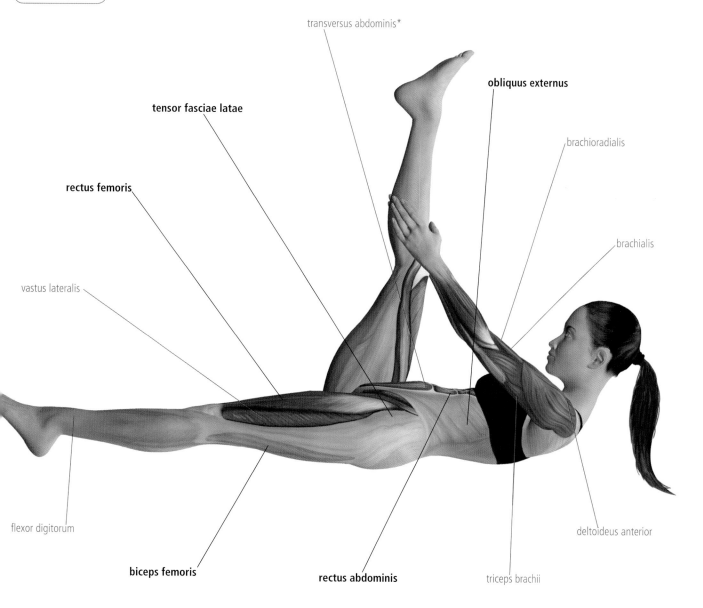

transversus abdominis*

obliquus externus

tensor fasciae latae

brachioradialis

rectus femoris

brachialis

vastus lateralis

flexor digitorum

deltoideus anterior

biceps femoris

rectus abdominis

triceps brachii

BOAT POSE

CORE STRENGTH & STABILITY

1 Sit on the floor. Lean back slightly, bending your knees, and support yourself with your hands behind your hips.

2 Exhale, and lift your feet off the floor as you lean back from your shoulders. Find your balance point between your sit bones and your tailbone.

3 Slowly straighten your legs in front of you so that they form a 45-degree angle with your torso. Extend your arms, and point your toes.

4 Pull your abdominals in toward your spine as they work to keep your balance. Stretch your arms forward through your fingertips, and elongate the back of your neck.

5 Hold for 10 to 20 seconds.

TARGETS
- Abdominals, including obliques
- Hip flexors
- Hamstrings
- Back muscles

BENEFITS
- Strengthens abdominals, hip flexors, spine, and thighs
- Stretches hamstrings
- Stimulates digestion
- May help to alleviate thyroid problems

NOT ADVISABLE IF YOU HAVE
- Headache
- Lower-back pain
- Neck injury

LOOK FOR
- Your neck to stay elongated and relaxed, minimizing tension in your upper spine.

BEST FOR
- rectus abdominis
- obliquus internus
- obliquus externus
- iliopsoas
- transversus abdominis
- vastus intermedius
- rectus femoris
- erector spinae

AVOID
- Allowing your abdominals to bulge outward; instead, keep them engaged, pressing your navel toward your spine.

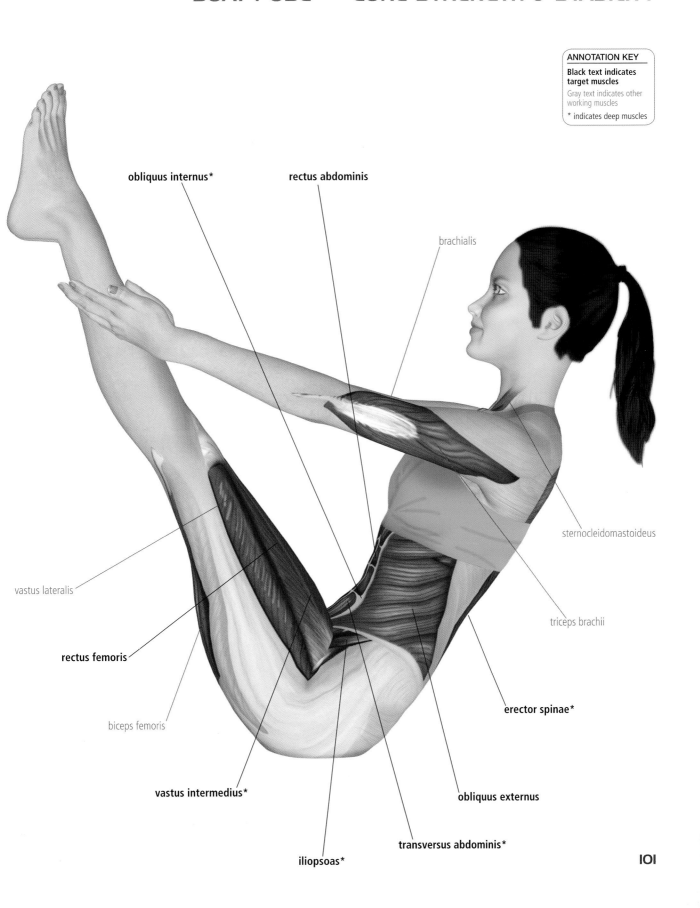

obliquus internus*

rectus abdominis

brachialis

vastus lateralis

rectus femoris

biceps femoris

vastus intermedius*

iliopsoas*

transversus abdominis*

obliquus externus

erector spinae*

triceps brachii

sternocleidomastoideus

LEMON SQUEEZER

1 Lie supine on the floor. Lift your legs, head, neck, and shoulders slightly off the floor, being careful not to arch your lower back. Your arms should be raised and parallel to the floor.

AVOID
• Allowing your shoulders to lift up toward your ears.

TARGETS
• Abdominals

BENEFITS
• Increases abdominal endurance
• Strengthens hip flexors

NOT ADVISABLE IF YOU HAVE
• Lower-back pain

2 Pulling your knees in toward your chest, reach your arms forward to your ankles, so that your torso lifts completely off the floor.

3 Slowly open up, lengthening your legs and lowering your torso back to the starting position.

4 Repeat the motion without completely lying down on the mat. Repeat fifteen times for two sets.

LOOK FOR
• Your chin to remain tucked.
• Your thigh muscles to be firm throughout the exercise.

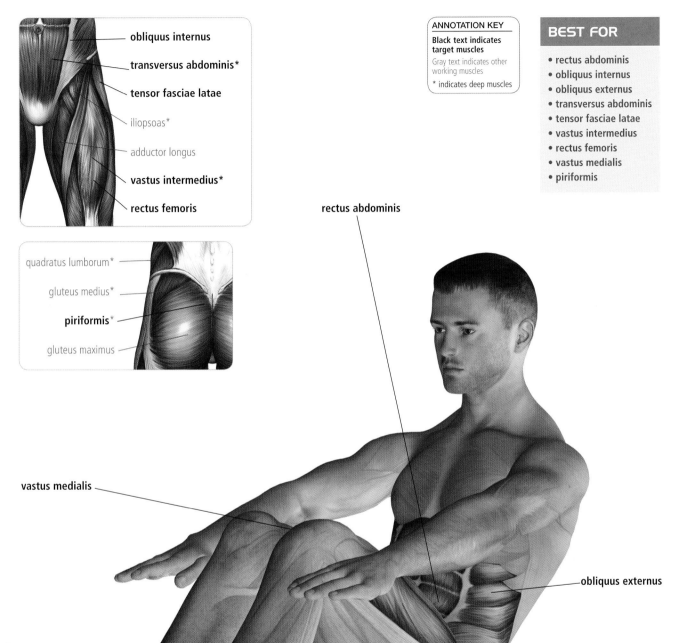

obliquus internus

transversus abdominis*

tensor fasciae latae

iliopsoas*

adductor longus

vastus intermedius*

rectus femoris

quadratus lumborum*

gluteus medius*

piriformis*

gluteus maximus

ANNOTATION KEY
Black text indicates
target muscles
Gray text indicates other
working muscles
* indicates deep muscles

BEST FOR

- rectus abdominis
- obliquus internus
- obliquus externus
- transversus abdominis
- tensor fasciae latae
- vastus intermedius
- rectus femoris
- vastus medialis
- piriformis

rectus abdominis

vastus medialis

obliquus externus

vastus lateralis

PLANK KNEE PULL-IN

1 Start in the plank position, with your shoulders directly over your hands, your torso straight.

BEST FOR

- rectus abdominis
- transversus abdominis
- sartorius
- obliquus externus
- rectus femoris
- tibialis anterior

2 Draw your left knee into your chest, flexing the foot while rocking your body forward over your hands. You should come up on the toes of your right foot.

TARGETS
- Scapular and core stabilisers
- Calf and hamstring flexibility

BENEFITS
- Improves posture and cores stability
- Increases calf and hamstring flexibility
- Strengthens abdominals

NOT ADVISABLE IF YOU HAVE
- Sharp lower-back pain
- Wrist pain
- Ankle pain

LOOK FOR
- Your shoulders to align over your hands and your toes to flex during the inward movement.

3 Extend your left knee backward, rocking the body back, and shifting your weight onto your heel. With your head in between your hands, straighten your right leg and lift it toward the ceiling. Repeat ten times on each leg.

AVOID
- Bending the knee of your supporting leg.

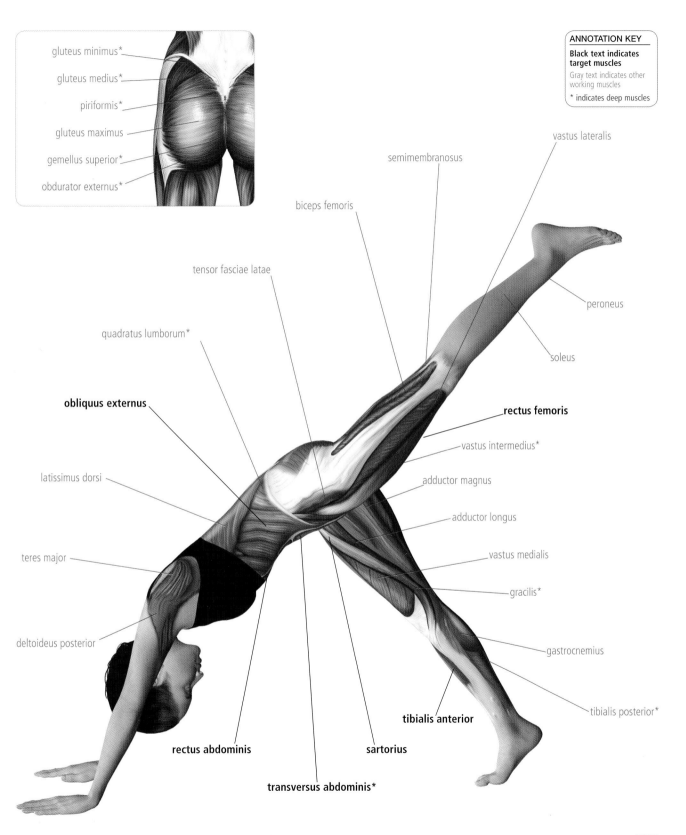

ANNOTATION KEY

Black text indicates target muscles

Gray text indicates other working muscles

* indicates deep muscles

gluteus minimus*

gluteus medius*

piriformis*

gluteus maximus

gemellus superior*

obdurator externus*

semimembranosus

biceps femoris

tensor fasciae latae

quadratus lumborum*

obliquus externus

latissimus dorsi

teres major

deltoideus posterior

rectus abdominis

transversus abdominis*

sartorius

tibialis anterior

vastus lateralis

peroneus

soleus

rectus femoris

vastus intermedius*

adductor magnus

adductor longus

vastus medialis

gracilis*

gastrocnemius

tibialis posterior*

V-UP

1 Lie on your back with your legs raised at an angle between 45 and 90 degrees.

2 Inhale, reaching your arms toward the ceiling as you lift your head and shoulders off the floor.

3 Exhale, and, while rolling through the spine, lift your rib cage off the floor to just before the sit bones.

LOOK FOR
- Articulation through the spine on the way up and on the way down.
- Your neck to remain elongated and relaxed, minimizing the tension in your upper spine.

TARGETS
- Abdominals

BENEFITS
- Strengthens abdominals while mobilising spine

NOT ADVISABLE IF YOU HAVE
- Advanced osteoporosis
- A herniated disc
- Lower-back pain

4 Inhale, and reach your arms toward your toes while maintaining a C curve in your back. Exhale, and roll down the spine by articulating one vertebra at a time. Return to the starting position.

AVOID
- Using momentum to carry you through the exercise. Use your abdominal muscles to lift your legs and torso.

BEST FOR
- rectus abdominis
- tensor fasciae latae
- rectus femoris
- vastus lateralis
- vastus medialis
- vastus intermedius
- adductor longus
- pectineus
- brachialis

ANNOTATION KEY

Black text indicates target muscles

Gray text indicates other working muscles

* indicates deep muscles

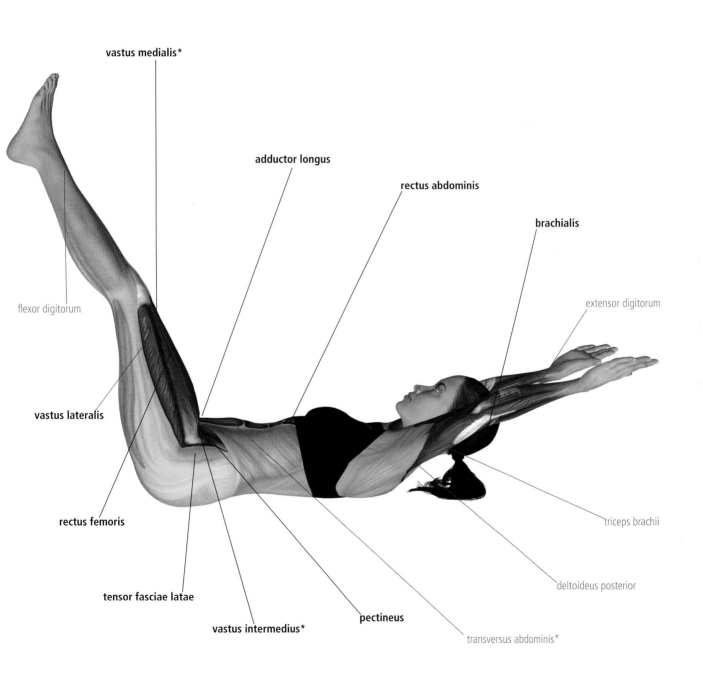

vastus medialis*

adductor longus

rectus abdominis

brachialis

flexor digitorum

extensor digitorum

vastus lateralis

rectus femoris

triceps brachii

tensor fasciae latae

deltoideus posterior

vastus intermedius*

pectineus

transversus abdominis*

CERVICAL STARS

① Sit or stand, keeping your neck, shoulders, and torso straight. Keeping your chin level, look straight ahead.

② Imagine that there is a star in front of you with a vertical line, a horizontal line, and two diagonal lines. Trace the star shape with your head and neck by following the vertical line up and down three times.

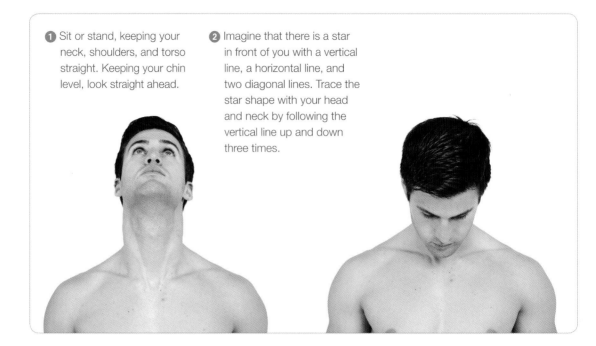

TARGETS
- Neck rotators
- Neck flexors
- Neck extensors
- Neck lateral flexors

BENEFITS
- Improves range of motion
- Relieves neck pain

NOT ADVISABLE IF YOU HAVE
- Numbness running down your arm or into your hand

③ Next, follow the horizontal line once.

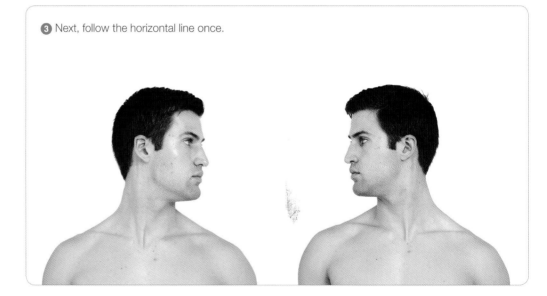

BEST FOR

- splenius
- sternocliedomastoideus
- levator scapulae
- scalenus
- semispinalis
- trapezius

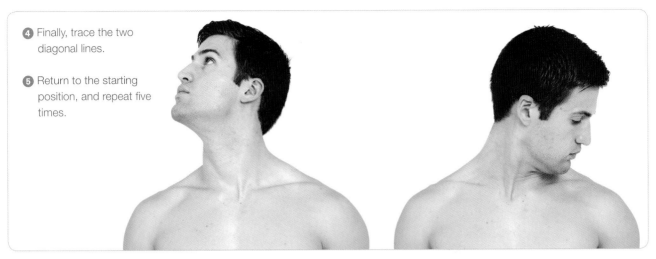

4 Finally, trace the two diagonal lines.

5 Return to the starting position, and repeat five times.

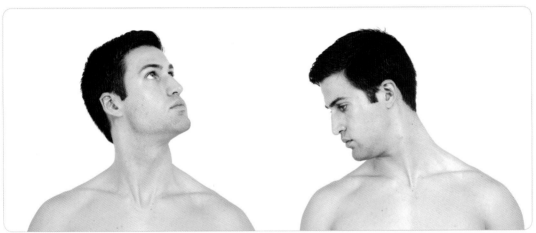

AVOID
• Hunching or tensing your shoulders.

ANNOTATION KEY
Black text indicates target muscles
Gray text indicates other working muscles
* indicates deep muscles

LOOK FOR
• Smooth, controlled movement.

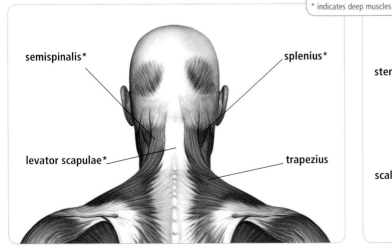

semispinalis*

splenius*

levator scapulae*

trapezius

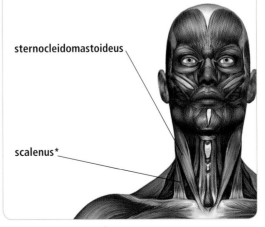

sternocleidomastoideus

scalenus*

BICYCLE

❶ Lie on your back with the roller placed lengthwise under your spine, your buttocks and shoulders resting on the roller. Place your forearms on the floor on either side of the roller to balance yourself.

❷ Draw your knees up to a tabletop position, forming a 90-degree angle between your hips, thighs, and calves.

LOOK FOR
- Your neck to remain relaxed throughout the exercise.
- Your leg to fully extend during the downward phase of the "pedalling" movement.

TARGETS
- Abdominals
- Thigh muscles

BENEFITS
- Improves pelvic stabilisation
- Strengthens abdominals

NOT ADVISABLE IF YOU HAVE
- Lower-back pain
- Neck pain

❸ Keeping your back flat, lift your head, neck, and shoulders off the roller. Straighten your right leg and pull your left knee in toward your chest, keeping your head, neck, and shoulders lifted.

❹ Switch legs while maintaining your balance, imitating the pedalling of a bike. Repeat fifteen times on each leg.

BEST FOR

- rectus abdominis
- transversus abdominis
- obliquus internus
- obliquus externus
- triceps brachii
- vastus intermedius
- rectus femoris
- vastus medialis

AVOID
- Allowing your shoulders to lift toward your ears.
- Lifting your hips and lower back during the movement.

ANNOTATION KEY
Black text indicates target muscles
Gray text indicates other working muscles
* indicates deep muscles

vastus intermedius*

vastus medialis

rectus femoris

rectus abdominis

vastus lateralis

obliquus internus*

obliquus externus

semimembranosus

biceps femoris

semitendinosus

adductor magnus

triceps brachii

iliopsoas*

transversus abdominis*

sartorius

tensor fasciae latae*

ADDUCTOR STRETCH

1 Standing, separate your feet wider than hip width, so that you are in a straddle position. Bend your knees.

2 Place your hands on your knees and bend at your hips, keeping your spine in neutral and your shoulders slightly forward.

AVOID
- Rounding your spine.
- Allowing your feet to shift or lift off the floor.
- Allowing your knees to extend over your toes while bending.

3 Keeping your torso in the same position and your hips behind your heels, shift your weight to one side, bending your knee while extending your opposite leg. Hold for 10 seconds and repeat on the other side.

TARGETS
- Hip adductors
- Hamstrings
- Gluteal muscles

BENEFITS
- Stretches hips, hamstrings, and gluteal muscles

NOT ADVISABLE IF YOU HAVE
- Hip injury
- Knee injury

LOOK FOR
- Your trunk to remain aligned as you move from side to side.
- Your hand placement on your thighs to assist your posture.
- Your neck and shoulders to remain relaxed.

ANNOTATION KEY
Black text indicates target muscles
Gray text indicates other working muscles
* indicates deep muscles

piriformis*

adductor magnus

semitendinosus

biceps femoris

semimembranosus

BEST FOR
- adductor longus
- adductor magnus
- peroneus
- biceps femoris
- semitendinosus
- semimembranosus
- piriformis

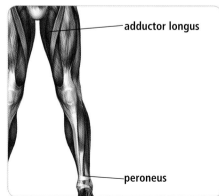

adductor longus

peroneus

HIP-TO-THIGH STRETCH

1 Kneeling on your left knee, place your right foot on the floor in front of you so that your right knee is bent less than 90 degrees.

2 Bring your torso forward, bending your right knee so that your knee shifts toward your toes. Keeping your torso in neutral position, press your right hip forward and downward to create a stretch over the front of your thigh. Raise your arms up toward the ceiling, keeping your shoulders relaxed.

3 Bring your arms down and move your hips backward. Straighten your right leg, and bring your torso forward. Place your hands on either side of your straight leg for support.

4 Hold for 10 seconds, and repeat the forward and backward movement five times on each leg.

TARGETS
- Thigh muscles
- Hip adductors

BENEFITS
- Stretches thigh muscles
- Stretches and improves range of motion in hips

NOT ADVISABLE IF YOU HAVE
- Knee injury

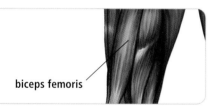

biceps femoris

AVOID
- Extending your front knee too far over the planted foot.
- Rotating your hips.
- Shifting the knee of the back leg outward.

LOOK FOR
- Your shoulders and neck to remain relaxed.
- Your entire body to move as one unit as you go into the stretch.

ANNOTATION KEY
Black text indicates target muscles
Gray text indicates other working muscles
* indicates deep muscles

BEST FOR
- iliopsoas
- biceps femoris
- rectus femoris

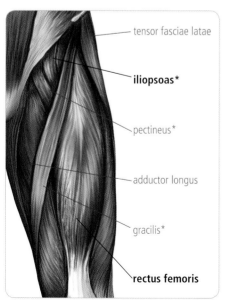

- tensor fasciae latae
- **iliopsoas***
- pectineus*
- adductor longus
- gracilis*
- **rectus femoris**

MODIFICATION
More difficult: During the backward movement, raise your back knee off the floor and straighten your back leg. Keep your hands on the floor.

HIP STRETCH

CORE STRENGTH & STABILITY

1. In a seated position, extend your left leg straight in front of you, and bend your right knee. Cross your bent knee over the straight leg, and keep your foot flat on the ground.

2. Wrap your left arm around the bent knee so that you are able to apply pressure to your leg to rotate your torso. Place your right hand on the floor for stability.

3. Keeping your hips aligned, rotate your upper spine as you pull your chest in toward your knee.

4. Hold for 30 seconds. Slowly release, and repeat five times on each side.

LOOK FOR
- Your neck and shoulders to remain relaxed.
- Your active hand to apply even pressure to your leg.
- Your torso to remain upright as you pull your knee and torso together.

TARGETS
- Oblique muscles
- Hip muscles
- Lower back
- Gluteal muscles

BENEFITS
- Stretches hips, gluteal muscles, and obliques

NOT ADVISABLE IF YOU HAVE
- Hip injury

AVOID
- Rounding your torso.
- Lifting the foot of your bent leg off the floor.
- Straining your neck as you rotate.

ANNOTATION KEY
Black text indicates target muscles
Gray text indicates other working muscles
* indicates deep muscles

BEST FOR
- obliquus internus
- obliquus externus
- quadratus lumborum
- multifidus spinae
- tractus iliotibialis
- gluteus maximus
- gluteus medius
- piriformis

latissimus dorsi

multifidus spinae*

quadratus lumborum*

gluteus medius*

piriformis*

tractus iliotibialis

gluteus maximus

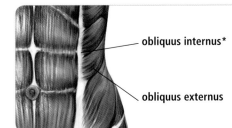

obliquus internus*

obliquus externus

PECTORAL STRETCH

1. Stand straight with your arms behind your back and your hands clasped together.

2. Pinch your shoulder blades together as you reach and lift your arms away from your body, making sure to keep your elbows straight.

AVOID
- Leaning your trunk too far forward while stretching—this can be harmful to your back.

BEST FOR
- pectoralis major
- pectoralis minor
- deltoids
- biceps brachii

TARGETS
- Shoulders
- Biceps
- Pectoral muscles

BENEFITS
- Stretches shoulders, biceps, and chest muscles

NOT ADVISABLE IF YOU HAVE
- Shoulder injury

LOOK FOR
- Your elbows to remain straight during the movement.
- Your palms to be turned outward while you lift your arms. This will intensify the stretch.

- deltoideus medialis
- deltoideus anterior
- pectoralis minor*
- pectoralis major
- biceps brachii

ANNOTATION KEY
Black text indicates target muscles
Gray text indicates other working muscles
* indicates deep muscles

115

PLANK ROLL-DOWN

AVOID
- Bending your knees or spine.
- Allowing your elbows to bend.

LOOK FOR
- Your spine and legs to remain straight.
- A slow, steady movement.
- Your abdominals to remain up and in.

① Stand tall with your weight equally distributed between your feet.

② Relaxing your neck, bend from your waist and bring your hands down toward the floor. Place them in front of your feet so that they are flat on the floor.

③ Walk your hands away from your feet until your body reaches a plank position, forming a straight line from your shoulders to your heels.

④ Keeping your arms straight, dip your shoulders three times while maintaining the plank position.

⑤ Walk your hands back to your feet, and return to an upright position. Repeat ten times at a rapid pace.

TARGETS
- Pectoral muscles
- Upper-arm muscles

BENEFITS
- Stabilises core
- Strengthens abdominals

NOT ADVISABLE IF YOU HAVE
- Wrist pain
- Shoulder issues
- Lower-back pain

MODIFICATION
Easier: Roll down to a plank position on your elbows, rather than on your hands. Supporting your torso with your forearms and maintaining the plank position, dip up and down three times.

PLANK ROLL-DOWN • CORE STRENGTH & STABILITY

- latissimus dorsi
- quadratus lumborum*
- rhomboideus*
- teres major
- gluteus maximus
- **deltoideus posterior**
- tensor fasciae latae
- **trapezius**
- **vastus lateralis**
- gastrocnemius
- selous
- **obliquus externus**
- **brachialis**
- **rectus femoris**
- tibialis anterior
- **triceps brachii**
- **biceps brachii**
- peroneus

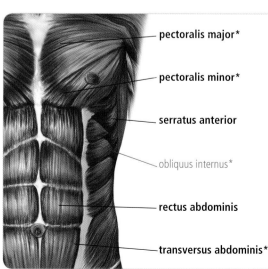

- **pectoralis major***
- **pectoralis minor***
- **serratus anterior**
- obliquus internus*
- **rectus abdominis**
- **transversus abdominis***

BEST FOR

- pectoralis major
- pectoralis minor
- rectus abdominis
- biceps brachii
- triceps brachii
- deltoideus posterior
- vastus lateralis
- transversus abdominis
- obliquus externus
- rectus femoris
- tibialis anterior
- brachialis
- serratus anterior
- trapezius

COBRA

❶ Lie facedown, legs extended behind you with toes pointed. Position the palms of your hands on the floor slightly above your shoulders, and rest your elbows on the floor.

TARGETS
• Abdominals

BENEFITS
• Strengthens spine and buttocks
• Stretches chest, abdominals, and shoulders

NOT ADVISABLE IF YOU HAVE
• Back injury

❷ Push down into the floor, and slowly lift through the top of your chest as you straighten your arms.

❸ Pull your tailbone down toward your pubis as you push your shoulders down and back.

❹ Elongate your neck and gaze forward.

AVOID
• Tipping your head too far backward.
• Overdoing this stretch—it can lead to excessive pressure on your lower back.

LOOK FOR
• A feeling of slight pressure between your hips and the floor.
• Your shoulders to remain relaxed, pressed down and away from your ears.

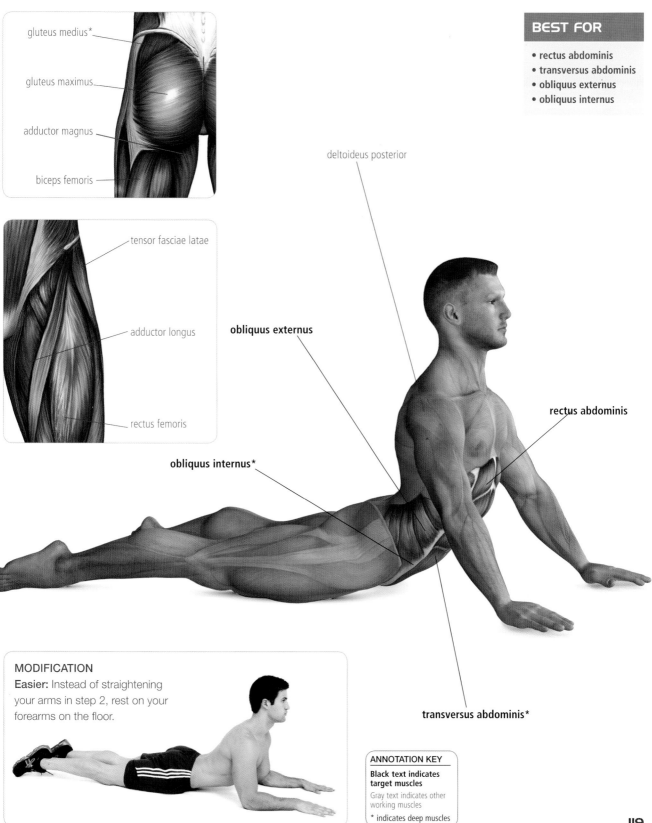

BEST FOR

- rectus abdominis
- transversus abdominis
- obliquus externus
- obliquus internus

gluteus medius*

gluteus maximus

adductor magnus

biceps femoris

tensor fasciae latae

adductor longus

rectus femoris

deltoideus posterior

obliquus externus

rectus abdominis

obliquus internus*

transversus abdominis*

MODIFICATION

Easier: Instead of straightening your arms in step 2, rest on your forearms on the floor.

ANNOTATION KEY

Black text indicates target muscles

Gray text indicates other working muscles

* indicates deep muscles

QUADRUPED LEG LIFT

1 Kneeling on all fours, connect with your abdominals by drawing your navel up toward your spine.

TARGETS
- Core stability
- Pelvic stabilisers
- Hip extensor muscles
- Oblique muscles

BENEFITS
- Tones arms, legs, and abdominals

NOT ADVISABLE IF YOU HAVE
- Wrist pain
- Lower-back pain
- Knee pain while kneeling
- Inability to stabilise the spine while moving limbs

2 Slowly raise your right arm and extend your left leg, all while keeping your torso still. Extend your arm and leg until they are both parallel to the floor, creating one long line with your body. Do not allow your pelvis to bend or rotate.

3 Bring your arm and leg back into the starting position.

4 Repeat sequence on the other side, alternating sides

LOOK FOR
- Your movement to be slow and steady to decrease pelvic rotation.

AVOID
- Tilting your pelvis during the movement— slide your leg along the surface of the floor before lifting.
- Allowing your back to sink into an arched position.

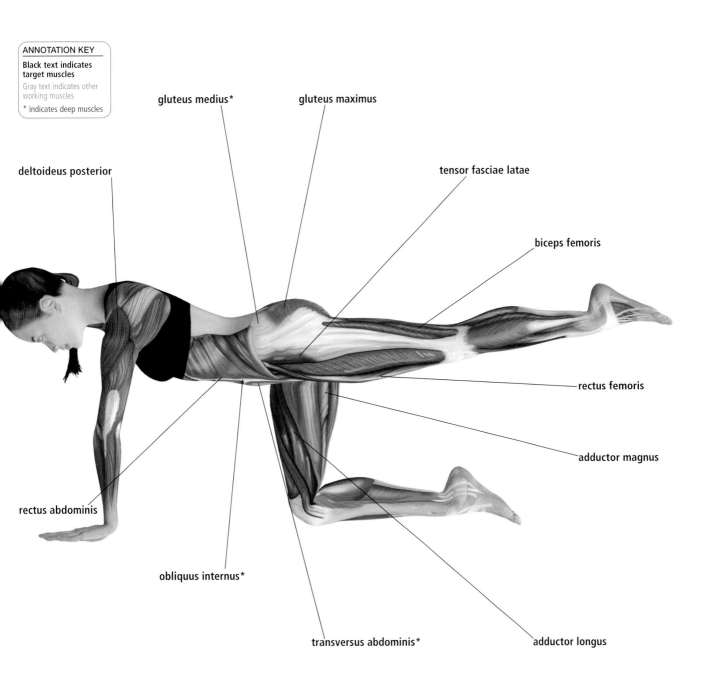

ANNOTATION KEY

Black text indicates target muscles

Gray text indicates other working muscles

* indicates deep muscles

gluteus medius*

gluteus maximus

deltoideus posterior

tensor fasciae latae

biceps femoris

rectus femoris

adductor magnus

rectus abdominis

obliquus internus*

transversus abdominis*

adductor longus

MODIFICATION
More difficult:
Instead of kneeling, press into a plank position to begin, and then raise the opposite arm and leg.

BEST FOR

- gluteus maximus
- biceps femoris
- gluteus medius
- deltoideus posterior
- adductor magnus
- rectus abdominis

- transversus abdominis
- obliquus internus
- tensor fasciae latae
- adductor longus
- rectus femoris

CROSSOVER CRUNCH

CORE STRENGTH & STABILITY

1 Bring your hands behind your head, lifting your legs off the floor into a tabletop position.

LOOK FOR
- Your neck to remain long and your chin to remain away from your chest.
- Both hips to remain stable on the floor.

2 Roll up with your torso, reaching your right elbow to your left knee and extending the right leg in front of you. Imagine pulling your shoulder blades off the floor and twisting from your ribs and oblique muscles.

3 Alternate sides. Repeat sequence six times.

TARGETS
- Torso stability
- Abdominals

BENEFITS
- Stabilises core
- Strengthens abdominals

NOT ADVISABLE IF YOU HAVE
- Neck issues
- Lower-back pain

AVOID
- Pulling with your hands, bringing your chin toward your chest, or arching your back.
- Moving the active elbow faster than your shoulder.

MODIFICATION
Easier: Begin with both feet on the floor. Place the outside of one foot on top of your thigh near your knee. Reach your opposite elbow toward the knee of your raised leg. After six repetitions, repeat on the other side.

ANNOTATION KEY

Black text indicates target muscles

Gray text indicates other working muscles

* indicates deep muscles

BEST FOR

- rectus abdominis
- transversus abdominis
- obliquus externus
- obliquus internus
- rectus femoris
- vastus medialis
- sartorius
- tensor fasciae latae

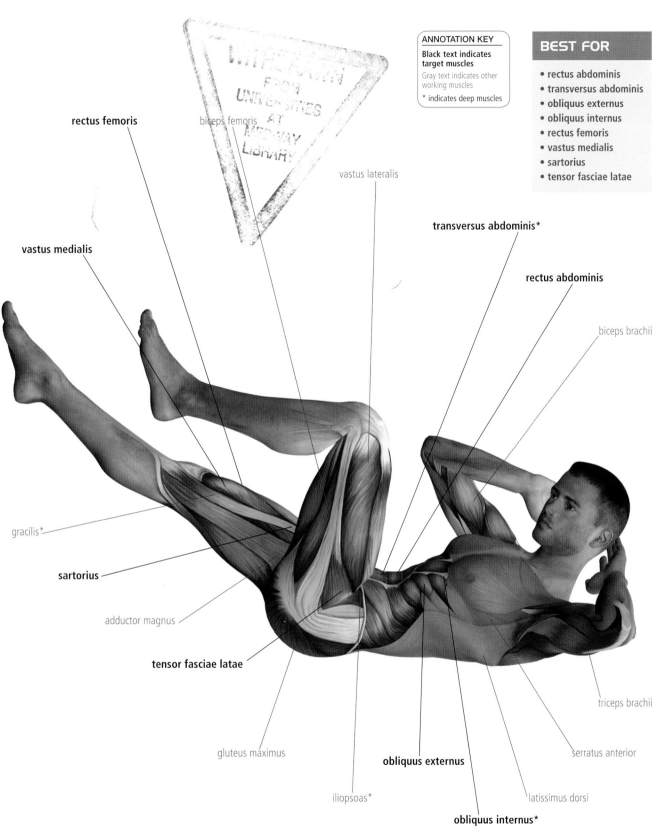

rectus femoris

biceps femoris

vastus lateralis

transversus abdominis*

rectus abdominis

biceps brachii

vastus medialis

gracilis*

sartorius

adductor magnus

tensor fasciae latae

triceps brachii

gluteus maximus

obliquus externus

serratus anterior

iliopsoas*

latissimus dorsi

obliquus internus*

ABDOMINAL HIP LIFT

LOOK FOR
- Your legs to remain straight and firm throughout the exercise.
- Your neck and shoulders to be relaxed as you lift the hips.

AVOID
- Jerking your movements or using momentum to lift the hips.

① Lie down with your legs in the air and crossed at the ankles, knees straight. Place your arms on the floor, straight by your sides.

TARGETS
- Abdominals
- Triceps

BENEFITS
- Strengthens core and pelvic stabilisers
- Firms and tones lower abdominals

NOT ADVISABLE IF YOU HAVE
- Back pain
- Neck pain
- Shoulder pain

② Pinching your legs together and squeezing your buttocks, press into the back of your arms to lift your hips upward.

③ Slowly return your hips to the floor. Repeat ten times, then switch with the opposite leg crossed in the front.

BEST FOR

- **rectus abdominis**
- **transversus abdominis**
- **vastus intermedius**
- **tensor fasciae latae**
- **gluteus maximus**
- **gluteus medius**
- **triceps brachii**
- **rectus femoris**
- **iliopsoas**

MODIFICATION
More difficult: Keeping your hips on the floor, raise your arms toward the ceiling. Reach toward your toes as you lift your shoulders off the floor.

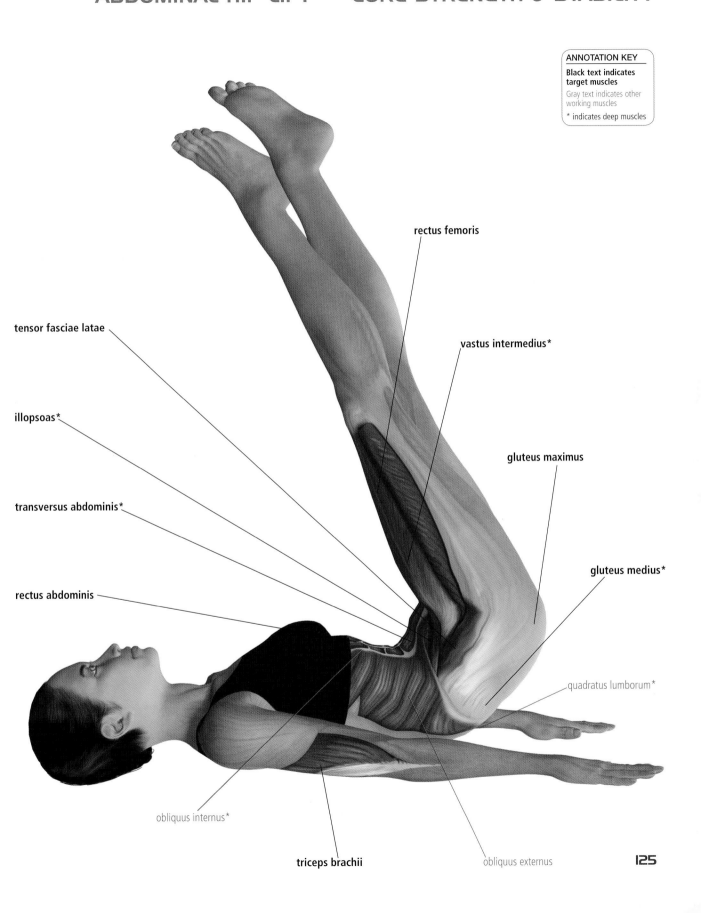

rectus femoris

tensor fasciae latae

vastus intermedius*

illopsoas*

gluteus maximus

transversus abdominis*

gluteus medius*

rectus abdominis

quadratus lumborum*

obliquus internus*

triceps brachii

obliquus externus

THE DEAD BUG

1. Lie on your back with the roller placed lengthwise under your spine, your buttocks and shoulders resting on the roller. Place your hands and forearms flat on the floor for stabilisation. Draw your knees up so that your legs form a tabletop-like position.

2. Lift your head, neck, and shoulders.

TARGETS
- Abdominals
- Leg muscles

BENEFITS
- Improves pelvic and core stabilisation
- Strengthens abdominals

NOT ADVISABLE IF YOU HAVE
- Lower-back pain
- Neck pain

3. Press the palms of your hands onto your knees, creating your own resistance as you try to balance. Flex your toes and keep your elbows pulled in to your sides. Hold for 10 seconds. Repeat ten times.

AVOID
- Hunching your shoulders.
- Lifting your hips or lower back during the movement.

LOOK FOR
- Your hips, thighs, and calves to form a 90-degree angle.
- Your neck to remain relaxed throughout the exercise.
- Your shoulders and buttocks to remain flat on the roller throughout the exercise.

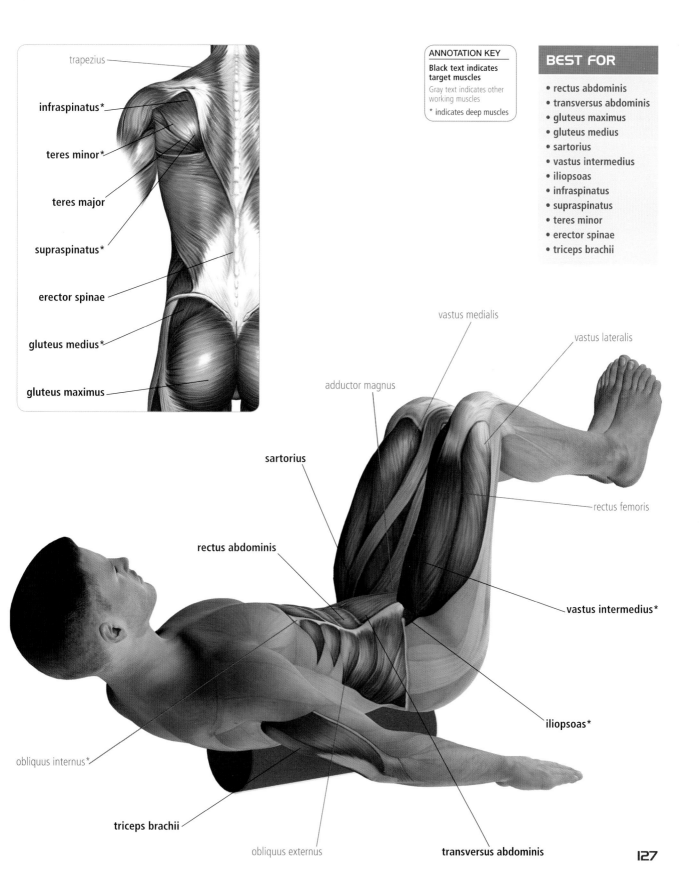

ANNOTATION KEY

Black text indicates target muscles

Gray text indicates other working muscles

* indicates deep muscles

BEST FOR

- rectus abdominis
- transversus abdominis
- gluteus maximus
- gluteus medius
- sartorius
- vastus intermedius
- iliopsoas
- infraspinatus
- supraspinatus
- teres minor
- erector spinae
- triceps brachii

trapezius

infraspinatus*

teres minor*

teres major

supraspinatus*

erector spinae

gluteus medius*

gluteus maximus

vastus medialis

vastus lateralis

adductor magnus

rectus femoris

sartorius

rectus abdominis

vastus intermedius*

iliopsoas*

obliquus internus*

triceps brachii

obliquus externus

transversus abdominis

BALANCE & POSTURE

Exercises that improve balance and posture will enhance the positive effects of your strengthening, stretching, and stabilising moves. These exercises bring multiple parts of the body into play; the goal is harmonious, centred movement that comes from a solid centre.

After all, cyclists need to consider so much more than developing leg strength. Many of the exercises that follow will build back strength and stability. An exercise like Swimming, for instance, counterbalances forward flexion movements and is essential in counteracting the effects of sitting forward on your bike, holding handlebars for hours on end. And Rolling Like a Ball deeply works the abdominal muscles evenly as it deeply releases and massages the lower back, which so often troubles cyclists. Be patient as you explore these exercises. Over time, you will build a regimen that works for you.

ROLLING LIKE A BALL

1 Sitting with your legs bent and feet raised off the floor, find your balance point. Place your hands around the backs of your thighs.

AVOID
- Using your arm muscles to roll and balance your body.
- Allowing your feet to touch the ground.

LOOK FOR
- Your back to curve throughout the movement.
- Using your abdominals to maintain your balance.

TARGETS
- Abdominal muscles

BENEFITS
- Massages back muscles
- Enhances abdominal control

NOT ADVISABLE IF YOU HAVE
- Neck issues

2 Using your lower abdominals to lift your hips, roll back onto your shoulders.

3 Exhale, using your abdominals to roll up to your balance point. Keep your shoulders relaxed throughout the movement.

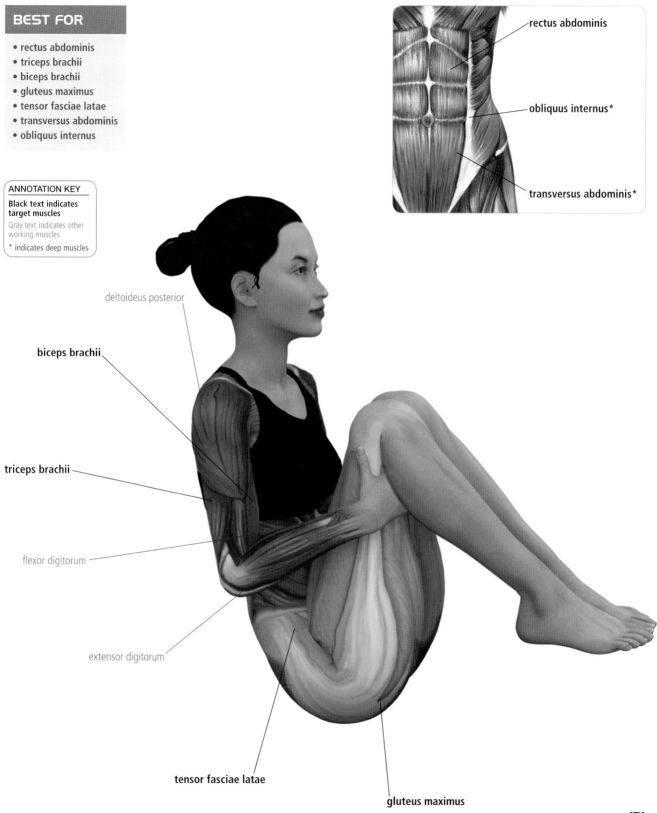

BEST FOR

- rectus abdominis
- triceps brachii
- biceps brachii
- gluteus maximus
- tensor fasciae latae
- transversus abdominis
- obliquus internus

ANNOTATION KEY

Black text indicates target muscles

Gray text indicates other working muscles

* indicates deep muscles

rectus abdominis

obliquus internus*

transversus abdominis*

deltoideus posterior

biceps brachii

triceps brachii

flexor digitorum

extensor digitorum

tensor fasciae latae

gluteus maximus

OPEN-LEG ROCKER

LOOK FOR
- Deeply scooped abdominal muscles.
- Your neck to stay elongated and relaxed.

AVOID
- Rolling back onto your neck. If you have trouble stopping, bend your knees slightly as you return to the starting position.

TARGETS
- Abdominal muscles
- Hip flexors

BENEFITS
- Develops stability in the spine through the rocking motion

NOT ADVISABLE IF YOU HAVE
- A herniated disc

1 Sitting on the mat, hold your legs or calves. Your legs should be abducted and parallel, with your knees straight.

2 Inhale, scooping your abdominals in while rolling off your sit bones. Do not allow your weight to extend beyond mid scapula.

3 Exhale, rolling your body back to the starting position. Repeat six to eight times.

BEST FOR

- rectus abdominis
- obliquus internus
- obliquus externus
- transversus abdominis
- iliopsoas

obliquus internus*

rectus abdominis

transversus abdominis*

obliquus externus

iliopsoas*

ANNOTATION KEY

Black text indicates
target muscles

Gray text indicates other
working muscles

* indicates deep muscles

TEASER I

❶ Lie on your back with your legs raised at an angle between 45 and 90 degrees.

❷ Inhale, reaching your arms toward the ceiling as you lift your head and shoulders off the mat.

TARGETS
• Abdominal muscles

BENEFITS
• Strengthens abdominals
• Mobilises spine

NOT ADVISABLE IF YOU HAVE
• Advanced osteoporosis
• A herniated disc
• Lower-back pain

LOOK FOR
• Articulation through your spine on the way up and on the way down.
• Your neck to stay elongated and relaxed, minimising tension in your upper spine.

❸ Exhale, and while rolling through the spine, lift your rib cage off the mat to just before the sit bones. At the same time, slowly lower your legs so that they are parallel to your arms.

❹ Inhale, raising the arms overhead while maintaining a C curve in your back. Exhale, rolling down the spine by articulating one vertebra at a time. Return to the starting position.

AVOID
• Using momentum to carry you through the exercise. Use your abdominal muscles to lift your legs and torso.

BEST FOR

- rectus abdominis
- tensor fasciae latae
- rectus femoris
- vastus lateralis
- vastus medialis
- vastus intermedius
- adductor longus
- pectineus
- brachialis

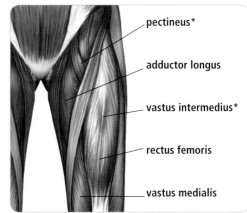

pectineus*

adductor longus

vastus intermedius*

rectus femoris

vastus medialis

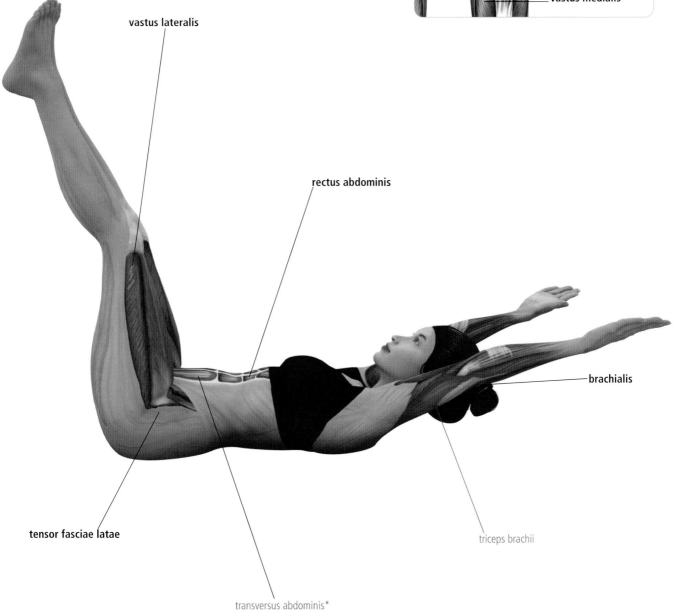

vastus lateralis

rectus abdominis

brachialis

tensor fasciae latae

triceps brachii

transversus abdominis*

TEASER II

① Lie down on your back, reaching your arms overhead. Your legs should be together and raised 45 to 90 degrees off the floor. Inhale to prepare.

LOOK FOR
• Stability in your upper body as you lift and lower your heels.
• Smooth, controlled movement.

TARGETS
• Abdominal muscles

BENEFITS
• Improves abdominal strength and endurance

NOT ADVISABLE IF YOU HAVE
• Lower-back pain

② Exhale, rolling up from your head through your spine one vertebra at a time until you are sitting just behind your sit bones, as in Teaser I.

③ Keeping your arms and upper body in position, slowly lower your heels and then raise them again. Repeat 3 to 5 times.

④ Lengthen your torso and exhale, rolling down the spine one vertebra at a time from the lumbar area of the spine to the top of your head.

AVOID
• Allowing your belly to bulge outward; instead, keep your core engaged and press your navel toward your spine.
• Hunching your shoulders.
• Compromising your form as you lift and lower your legs.

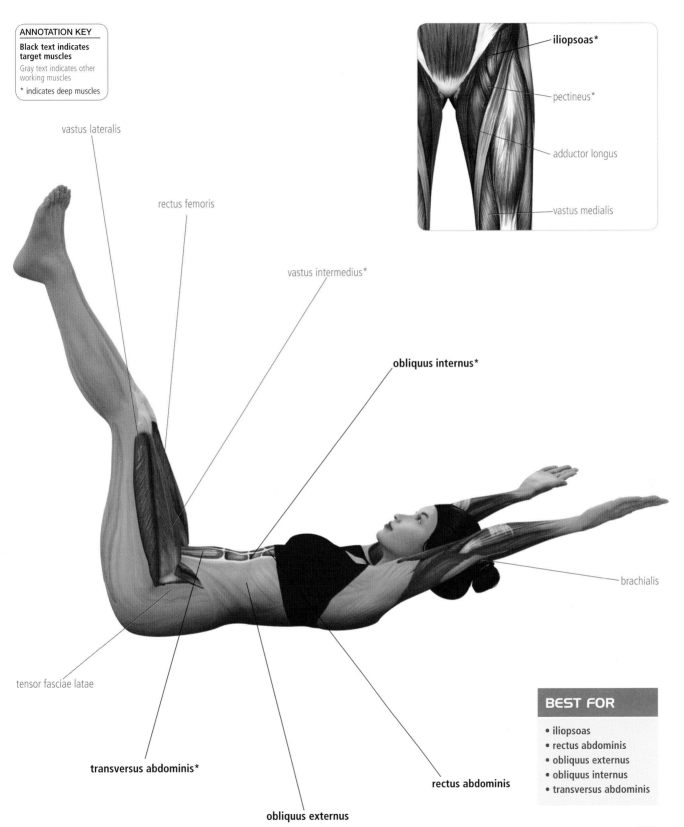

ANNOTATION KEY

Black text indicates target muscles

Gray text indicates other working muscles

* indicates deep muscles

iliopsoas*

pectineus*

adductor longus

vastus medialis

vastus lateralis

rectus femoris

vastus intermedius*

obliquus internus*

brachialis

tensor fasciae latae

transversus abdominis*

rectus abdominis

obliquus externus

BEST FOR

- iliopsoas
- rectus abdominis
- obliquus externus
- obliquus internus
- transversus abdominis

DOUBLE-LEG KICK

1 Lying prone on the floor with your legs adducted and parallel, flex your knees. Bend your arms and place your hands, interlaced, in the small of your back. Allow your elbows to drop down to the mat.

2 Exhale, pulsing your knees for three breaths while keeping your pelvis stable.

TARGETS
- Erector spinae
- Hip extensors

BENEFITS
- Opens chest
- Strengthens back
- Tones thighs and buttocks

NOT ADVISABLE IF YOU HAVE
- Cervical issues
- Sharp lower-back pain

3 Inhale, and stretch your spine and hips, separating your legs and reaching your arms back toward your hips. Look forward through the stretch. Extend your arms far behind your back, squeezing your shoulder blades together to open up your chest.

4 Exhale, bringing your legs together and bending your knees to return to your starting position. Bend your elbows and bring your hands to the small of your back.

5 Repeat the sequence five to six times.

AVOID
- Moving too quickly.
- Lifting hips off mat.

LOOK FOR
- Drawing your abdominals in toward your spine throughout the entire exercise.
- Your neck to stay elongated and relaxed.

ANNOTATION KEY

Black text indicates target muscles

Gray text indicates other working muscles

* indicates deep muscles

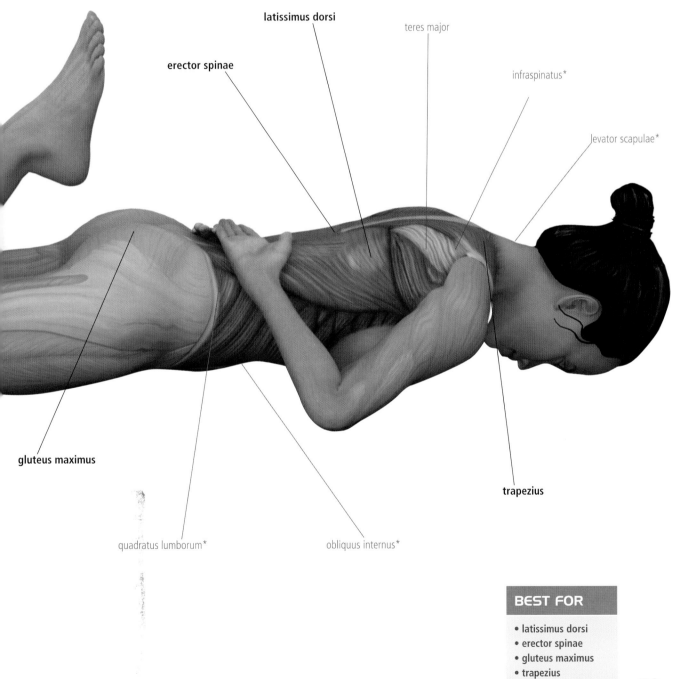

latissimus dorsi

erector spinae

teres major

infraspinatus*

levator scapulae*

gluteus maximus

trapezius

quadratus lumborum*

obliquus internus*

BEST FOR

- latissimus dorsi
- erector spinae
- gluteus maximus
- trapezius

SIDE MERMAID

① Sit to one side with your knees bent and your legs folded one on top of the other. Place your hand on your ankles. Inhale, reaching your other arm toward the ceiling.

LOOK FOR
• Reaching your arm far behind your body to open your chest and reach a maximum stretch.

② Exhale, reaching your arm in the direction of your ankles, pulling your navel toward your spine and rotating the torso slightly backward.

③ Inhale, returning to the starting position. Repeat on the other side.

TARGETS
• Abdominal muscles, including obliques

BENEFITS
• Stretches spine and entire torso
• Opens up chest and tight back muscles

NOT ADVISABLE IF YOU HAVE
• Intense back pain
• Hip pain rooted deeply in the joints

AVOID
• Knee pain in the initial position. If you experience pain, you can sit on a pillow or straighten your top leg to the side.

ANNOTATION KEY
Black text indicates target muscles
Gray text indicates other working muscles
* indicates deep muscles

BEST FOR

- rectus abdominis
- transversus abdominis
- obliquus internus
- obliquus externus
- latissimus dorsi

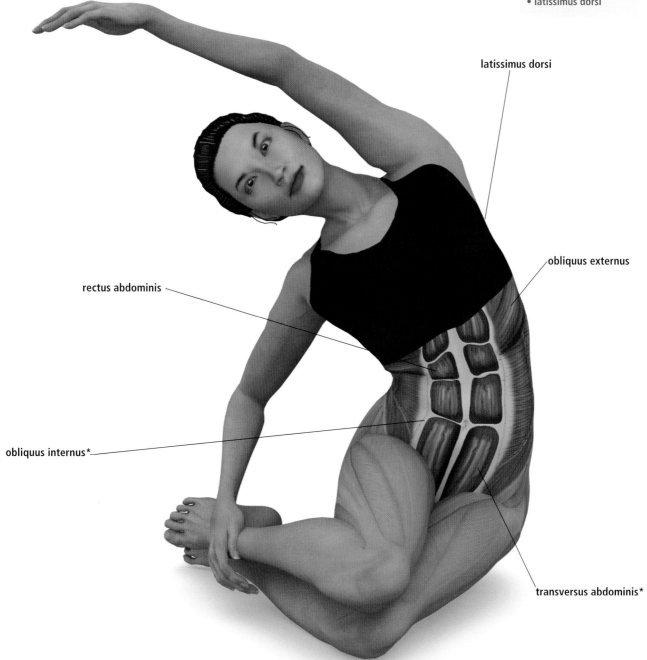

latissimus dorsi

obliquus externus

rectus abdominis

obliquus internus*

transversus abdominis*

PRONE HEEL BEATS

1. Lie facedown with your arms lifted off the floor by your hips, palms up. Draw your shoulders down away from your ears. Turn your legs out from the top of your hips and pull your inner thighs together.

2. Pull your navel off the mat and toward your spine, pressing your pubic bone into the mat. Lengthen your legs and lift them off the mat, tightening your thigh muscles.

3. Press your heels together and then separate them in a rapid but controlled motion.

4. Beat heels together for eight counts, then return to the starting position. Repeat sequence six to eight times.

TARGETS
- Core stabilisers

BENEFITS
- Encourages muscles from the entire body to work together
- Lengthens extension muscles

NOT ADVISABLE IF YOU HAVE
- Back pain

AVOID
- Tensing your shoulders.

LOOK FOR
- Your buttocks and your abdominals to be squeezed while beating your heels.
- Your breathing to remain steady.

BEST FOR

- trapezius
- latissimus dorsi
- teres major
- teres minor
- deltoideus posterior
- gluteus maximus
- biceps femoris
- adductor magnus
- soleus
- vastus lateralis

ANNOTATION KEY

Black text indicates target muscles

Gray text indicates other working muscles

* indicates deep muscles

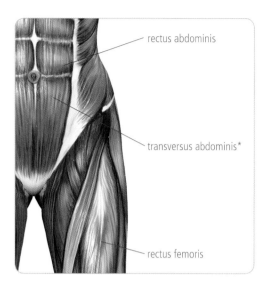

rectus abdominis

transversus abdominis*

rectus femoris

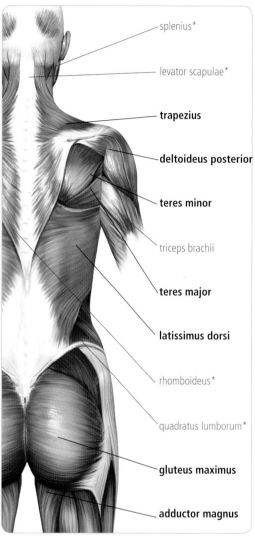

splenius*

levator scapulae*

trapezius

deltoideus posterior

teres minor

triceps brachii

teres major

latissimus dorsi

rhomboideus*

quadratus lumborum*

gluteus maximus

adductor magnus

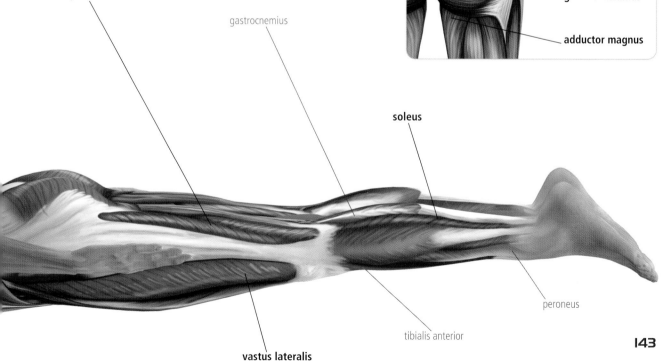

biceps femoris

gastrocnemius

soleus

peroneus

tibialis anterior

vastus lateralis

SWIMMING

1 Lie prone on the floor with your legs hip-width apart. Stretch your arms beside your ears on the floor. Engage your pelvic floor, and draw your navel toward your spine.

2 Extend through your upper back as you lift your left arm and right leg simultaneously. Lift your head and shoulders off the floor.

TARGETS
• Spinal extensors
• Hip extensors

BENEFITS
• Strengthens hip and spine extensors
• Challenges stabilisation of the spine against rotation

NOT ADVISABLE IF YOU HAVE
• Lower-back pain
• Extreme curvature of the upper spine
• Curvature of the lower spine

AVOID
• Allowing your shoulders to lift toward your ears.

LOOK FOR
• Your limbs to extend as long as possible in opposite directions.
• Your buttocks to remain tightly squeezed and your navel to be drawn into your spine throughout the exercise.
• Your neck to remain long and relaxed.

3 Lower your arm and leg to the starting position, maintaining a stretch in your limbs throughout.

4 Extend your right arm and left leg off the floor, lengthening and lifting your head and shoulders.

5 Elongate your limbs as you return to the starting position. Repeat six to eight times.

MODIFICATION

More difficult: Instead of lifting the opposite leg and arm, lift both arms and legs simultaneously, continuing to draw your navel into your spine. This version of the exercise is commonly known as Superman.

BEST FOR

- gluteus maximus
- biceps femoris
- erector spinae
- quadratus lumborum
- rhomboideus
- latissimus dorsi

ANNOTATION KEY

Black text indicates target muscles
Gray text indicates other working muscles
* indicates deep muscles

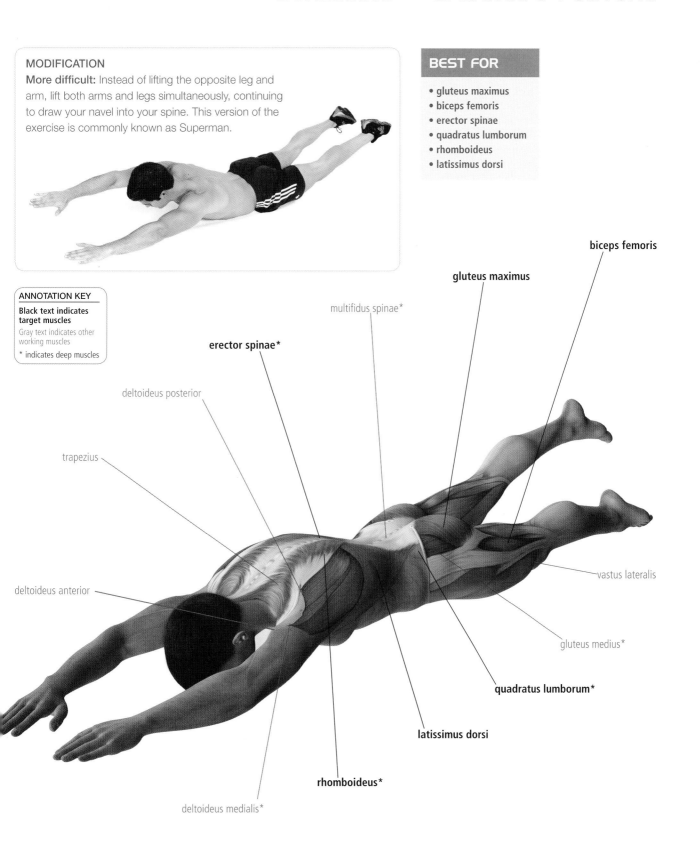

biceps femoris

gluteus maximus

multifidus spinae*

erector spinae*

deltoideus posterior

trapezius

deltoideus anterior

vastus lateralis

gluteus medius*

quadratus lumborum*

latissimus dorsi

rhomboideus*

deltoideus medialis*

WORKOUTS

The following workouts have been devised with two purposes in mind:
to help make you a better cyclist, and to keep your body balanced.
It's now time to put together what you've learned throughout this
book. Regardless of your fitness level, these workouts will benefit you.
For instance, the Healthy Back Workout will help protect you from
back fatigue on the bike, and the Balancing Workout will help develop
muscles to stabilise your core.

Before stretching, be sure to warm up, whether this involves a
brisk walk or some range-of-motion moves. Rest between exercises
if necessary, and remember that the quality of your movement often
matters more than the number of repetitions you perform. Pay close
attention to proper form, and you will find these workouts to be
valuable, plateau-defeating tools in your progression to cycling fitness.

BEGINNER'S WORKOUT

1 Iliotibial Band Stretch

page 43

2 Quadriceps Stretch

page 49

3 Lateral Low Lunge

pages 58–59

4 Single-Leg Circle

pages 82–83

5 Front Plank

pages 88–89

6 Bicycle

pages 110–111

7 Cobra

pages 118–119

8 Side Mermaid

pages 140–141

9 Prone Heel Beats

pages 142–143

INTERMEDIATE WORKOUT

❶ Spinal Twist

pages 26–27

❷ Chair Dip

pages 70–71

❸ Power Squat

pages 78–79

❹ Wall Sit

pages 68–69

❺ Scissors

pages 98–99

❻ Single-Leg kick

pages 96–97

❼ Push-Up

pages 72–73

❽ Hamstrings Stretch

pages 40–41

❾ Plank Press-Up

pages 94–95

❿ Plank Knee Pull-In

pages 104–105

ADVANCED WORKOUT

❶ Piriformis Stretch

page 35

❷ Thigh Rock-Back

pages 80–81

❸ Hip Flexor Stretch

page 32

❹ Lemon Squeezer

pages 102–103

❺ V-Up

pages 106–107

❻ Teaser I

pages 134–135

❼ Plank Press-Up

pages 94–95

❽ Hip-to-Thigh Stretch

page 113

❾ Roller Push-Up

pages 76–77

QUADRICEPS-STRENGTHENING WORKOUT

❶ Quadriceps Stretch

page 49

❷ Lateral Low Lunge

pages 58–59

❸ Wall Sit

pages 68–69

❹ Double-Leg Kick

pages 138–139

❺ Thigh Rock-Back

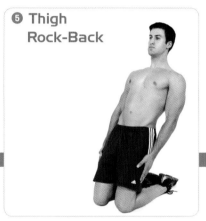

pages 80–81

❻ Adductor Stretch

page 112

❼ Butterfly Stretches

pages 52–53

❽ Clamshell Series

pages 84–85

HEALTHY BACK WORKOUT

❶ Upper and Lower Back Stretch

page 33

❷ Cervical Stars

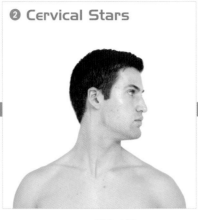

pages 108–109

❸ Forward Lunge

pages 60–61

❹ Lumbar Stretch

page 39

❺ Spine Stretch

page 38

❻ Scoop Rhomboids

page 34

❼ The Dead Bug

pages 126–127

❽ Prone Heel Beats

pages 142–143

❾ Rolling Like a Ball

pages 130–131

CORE-STABILISING WORKOUT

❶ Side Plank Balance

pages 90–91

❷ Abdominal Hip Lift

pages 124–125

❸ The Dead Bug

pages 126–127

❹ Bridge with Leg Lift

pages 64–65

❺ Hip Stretch

page 114

❻ Crossover Crunch

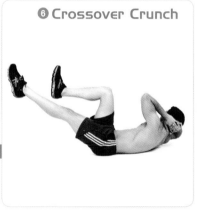

pages 122–123

❼ Teaser II

pages 136–137

❽ Swimming

pages 144–145

❾ Open-Leg Rocker

pages 132–133

LOW-IMPACT WORKOUT

❶ Side-Lying Knee Bend

pages 62–63

❷ Bicycle

pages 110–111

❸ Scissors

pages 98–99

❹ Front Plank

pages 88–89

❺ Hip Flexor Stretch

page 32

❻ Prone Heel Beats

pages 142–143

❼ Swimming

pages 144–145

❽ Abdominal Hip Lift

pages 124–125

❾ Crossover Crunch

pages 122–123

STAMINA CHALLENGE

❶ Roller Triceps Dip

pages 74–75

❷ Teaser I

pages 134–135

❸ Teaser II

pages 136–137

❹ Wall Sit

pages 68–69

❺ Quadruped Leg Lift

pages 120–121

❻ Plank Roll-Down

pages 116–117

❼ Forward Lunge

pages 60–61

❽ Push-Up

pages 72–73

❾ Pectoral Stretch

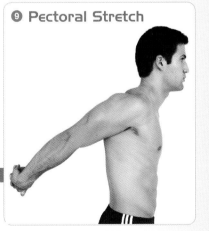

page 115

BALANCING WORKOUT

❶ Hip Flexor Stretch

page 32

❷ Power Squat

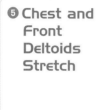

pages 78–79

❸ Swimming

pages 144–145

❹ Hand-to-Toe Lift

pages 44–45

❺ Chest and Front Deltoids Stretch

page 28

❻ Adductor Stretch

page 112

❼ Roller Push-Up

pages 76–77

❽ Bicycle

pages 110–111

❾ Plank Knee Pull-In

pages 104–105

❿ Quadruped Leg Lift

pages 120–121

POSTURAL WORKOUT

① Chest and Front Deltoids Stretch

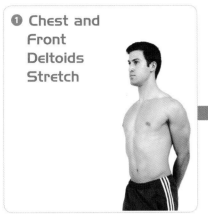

page 28

② Hand-to-Toe Lift

pages 44–45

③ Cobra

pages 118–119

④ Lying-Down Figure 4

pages 54–55

⑤ Boat Pose

pages 100–101

⑥ Rolling Like a Ball

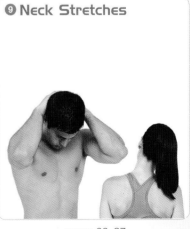

pages 130–131

⑦ Side Mermaid

pages 140–141

⑧ Teaser I

pages 134–135

⑨ Neck Stretches

pages 36–37

GLOSSARY OF MUSCULATURE

The following glossary explains the Latin terminology used to describe the body's musculature. Certain words are derived from Greek, which is indicated in each instance.

CHEST

coracobrachialis: Greek *korakoeidés*, "ravenlike," and *brachium*, "arm"

pectoralis (major and minor): *pectus*, "breast"

ABDOMEN

obliquus externus: *obliquus*, "slanting," and *externus*, "outward"

obliquus internus: *obliquus*, "slanting," and *internus*, "within"

rectus abdominis: *rego*, "straight, upright," and *abdomen*, "belly"

serratus anterior: *serra*, "saw," and *ante*, "before"

transversus abdominis: *transversus*, "athwart," and *abdomen*, "belly"

NECK

scalenus: Greek *skalénós*, "unequal"

semispinalis: *semi*, "half," and *spinae*, "spine"

splenius: Greek *splénion*, "plaster, patch"

sternocleidomastoideus: Greek *stérnon*, "chest," Greek *kleís*, "key," and Greek *mastoeidés*, "breastlike"

BACK

erector spinae: *erectus*, "straight," and *spina*, "thorn"

latissimus dorsi: *latus*, "wide," and *dorsum*, "back"

multifidus spinae: *multifid*, "to cut into divisions," and *spinae*, "spine"

quadratus lumborum: *quadratus*, "square, rectangular," and *lumbus*, "loin"

rhomboideus: Greek *rhembesthai*, "to spin"

trapezius: Greek *trapezion*, "small table"

SHOULDERS

deltoideus (anterior, medial, and posterior): Greek *deltoeidés*, "delta-shaped"

infraspinatus: *infra*, "under," and *spina*, "thorn"

levator scapulae: *levare*, "to raise," and *scapulae*, "shoulder [blades]"

subscapularis: *sub*, "below," and *scapulae*, "shoulder [blades]"

supraspinatus: *supra,* "above," and *spina*, "thorn"

teres (major and minor): *teres*, "rounded"

UPPER ARM

biceps brachii: *biceps*, "two-headed," and *brachium*, "arm"

brachialis: *brachium*, "arm"

triceps brachii: *triceps*, "three-headed," and *brachium*, "arm"

LOWER ARM

anconeus: Greek *anconad*, "elbow"

brachioradialis: *brachium*, "arm," and *radius*, "spoke"

extensor carpi radialis: *extendere*, "to extend," Greek *karpós*, "wrist," and *radius*, "spoke"

extensor digitorum: *extendere*, "to extend," and *digitus*, "finger, toe"

flexor carpi pollicis longus: *flectere*, "to bend," Greek *karpós*, "wrist," *pollicis*, "thumb," and *longus*, "long"

flexor carpi radialis: *flectere*, "to bend," Greek *karpós*, "wrist," and *radius*, "spoke"

flexor carpi ulnaris: *flectere*, "to bend," Greek *karpós*, "wrist," and *ulnaris*, "forearm"

flexor digitorum: *flectere*, "to bend," and *digitus*, "finger, toe"

palmaris longus: *palmaris*, "palm," and *longus*, "long"

pronator teres: *pronate*, "to rotate," and *teres*, "rounded.

HIPS

gemellus (inferior and superior): *geminus*, "twin"

gluteus maximus: Greek *gloutós*, "rump," and *maximus*, "largest"

gluteus medius: Greek *gloutós*, "rump," and *medialis*, "middle"

gluteus minimus: Greek *gloutós*, "rump," and *minimus*, "smallest"

iliopsoas: *ilium*, "groin," and Greek *psoa*, "groin muscle"

iliacus: *ilium*, "groin"

obturator externus: *obturare*, "to block," and *externus*, "outward"

obturator internus: *obturare*, "to block," and *internus*, "within"

pectineus: *pectin*, "comb"

piriformis: *pirum*, "pear," and *forma*, "shape"

quadratus femoris: *quadratus*, "square, rectangular," and *femur*, "thigh"

UPPER LEG

adductor longus: *adducere*, "to contract," and *longus*, "long"

adductor magnus: *adducere*, "to contract," and *magnus*, "major"

biceps femoris: *biceps*, "two-headed," and *femur*, "thigh"

gracilis: *gracilis*, "slim, slender"

rectus femoris: *rego*, "straight, upright," and *femur*, "thigh"

sartorius: *sarcio*, "to patch" or "to repair"

semimembranosus: *semi*, "half," and *membrum*, "limb"

semitendinosus: *semi*, "half," and *tendo*, "tendon"

tensor fasciae latae: *tenere*, "to stretch," *fasciae*, "band," and *latae*, "laid down"

vastus intermedius: *vastus*, "immense, huge," and *intermedius*, "between"

vastus lateralis: *vastus*, "immense, huge," and lateralis, "side"

vastus medialis: *vastus*, "immense, huge," and *medialis*, "middle"

LOWER LEG

adductor digiti minimi: *adducere*, "to contract," *digitus*, "finger, toe," and *minimum* "smallest"

adductor hallucis: *adducere*, "to contract," and *hallex*, "big toe"

extensor digitorum: *extendere*, "to extend," and *digitus*, "finger, toe"

extensor hallucis: *extendere*, "to extend," and *hallex*, "big toe"

flexor digitorum: *flectere*, "to bend," and *digitus*, "finger, toe"

flexor hallucis: *flectere*, "to bend," and *hallex*, "big toe"

gastrocnemius: Greek *gastroknémía*, "calf [of the leg]"

peroneus: *peronei*, "of the fibula"

plantaris: *planta*, "the sole"

soleus: *solea*, "sandal"

tibialis anterior: *tibia*, "reed pipe," and *ante*, "before"

tibialis posterior: *tibia*, "reed pipe," and *posterus*, "coming after"

trochlea tali: *trochleae*, "a pulley-shaped structure," and *talus*, "lower portion of ankle joint"

CREDITS & ACKNOWLEDGEMENTS

All photographs by FineArtsPhotoGroup.com, except the following: pages 10 sainthorant daniel; 14 Ron Kloberdanz/Shutterstock.com; 15 Fatseyeva/Shutterstock.com; 16 YanLev/Shutterstock.com; 17 top David Lee/Shutterstock.com; 17 middle Venus Angel/Shutterstock.com; 17 bottom Tatuasha/Shutterstock.com; 18 top left farvatar/Shutterstock; 18 top right Stefan Schurr/Shutterstock.com; 18 bottom left BKingFoto/Shutterstock; 18 bottom right Jo Crebbin/Shutterstock.com; and 160 Rich Pampin.

Models: David Anderson and Maria Grippi.

All large anatomical illustrations by Hector Aiza/3D Labz Animation India (www.3dlabz.com), with small insets by Linda Bucklin/Shutterstock.com.

ACKNOWLEDGEMENTS

My love of cycling gives me so many reasons to be thankful. Whether it's the selfless people I've met while raising money to fight cancer with Team Fatty or the inspired advocates from nonprofits across the country who empower cyclists to develop their passion, the amazing people whom I've met inspire me every single day. I want to thank my mother, Pat Useloff, for supporting me, helping me, and guiding me though absolutely everything in my life; I love you more than words, Mom. Thank you to all of my family for helping me make time to accomplish this book. Thank you to my photographer and friend, Rich Pampin, for the perfectly timed creative photography session; your talent amazes me. Thank you to my personal trainer, Andy Mei, who helped me understand so much about how the body works and how to keep balance in my training. Thank you to everyone at the Rockland Bicycling Club, League of American Bicyclists, and Bike New York, and to my riding partners, especially Daniel Berlinger for his unending friendship as well as Gerry Hoffberg who taught me that no matter how old you are, you can keep turning those pedals. Thank you especially to all my students for teaching me what you need, and how to help you achieve your goals. That knowledge went into every word of this book, helping others to achieve their goals, too. I'm humbled to have been part of your journey.

The author and publisher also offer thanks to those closely involved in the creation of this book: Moseley Road president Sean Moore, editor Erica Gordon-Mallin, and designer Danielle Scaramuzzo.

ABOUT THE AUTHOR

Jennifer Laurita is a League of American Bicyclists Instructor and national-level coach, training and certifying instructors across the United States in all aspects of bicycling. An avid year-round cyclist, she participates in charity events across the country. She has presented cycling education to the nation's largest educational conference, and uses her cycling experience as a basis for motivational speaking. She consults on development of bicycling programs, curricula, and event implementation, as well as presenting bicycling lessons to school districts, conducting staff development, and training Safe Routes to Schools coordinators through Rutgers University. She is also a founding member of the New Jersey Bike & Walk Coalition. A certified science teacher, Jennifer lives in northern New Jersey.

To my mother and my son, Gray.
I love you to the ends of the earth.